Health

Alvey Bohl

Public Health

General wellbeing, the craftsmanship and study of forestalling illness, drawing out life, and advancing physical and psychological well-being, sterilization, individual cleanliness, control of irresistible sicknesses, and association of wellbeing administrations. From the ordinary human collaborations associated with managing the numerous issues of public activity, there has arisen an acknowledgment of the significance of local area activity in the advancement of wellbeing and the counteraction and treatment of illness, and this is communicated in the idea of general wellbeing.

Tantamount expressions for general wellbeing medication are social medication and local area medication; the last option has been broadly embraced in the Assembled Realm, and the experts are called local area doctors. The act of general wellbeing draws vigorously on clinical science and reasoning and focuses particularly on controlling and controlling the climate to serve general society. It is concerned in this manner with lodging, water supplies, and food. Harmful specialists can be brought into these through cultivating, composts, deficient sewage removal and waste, development, faulty warming and ventilating frameworks, apparatus, and poisonous synthetics. General wellbeing medication is essential for the more prominent venture of saving and working on the general wellbeing. Local area doctors help out different gatherings, from planners, manufacturers, sterile and warming and ventilating specialists, and industrial facility and food auditors to analysts and sociologists, scientific experts, physicists, and toxicologists. Word related medication is worried about the wellbeing, security, and government assistance of people in the working environment. It very well might be seen as a specific piece of general wellbeing medication since its point is to diminish the dangers in the climate where people work.

The endeavor of safeguarding, keeping up with, and effectively advancing general wellbeing requires extraordinary techniques for data gathering (the study of disease transmission) and corporate plans to follow up on critical discoveries and set them up as a regular occurrence. Measurements gathered by disease transmission specialists endeavor to portray and make sense of the event of sickness in a populace by connecting variables like eating regimen, climate, radiation openness, or cigarette smoking with the occurrence and pervasiveness of illness. The public authority, through regulations and guidelines, makes organizations to administer and officially investigate and screen water supplies, food handling, sewage treatment, channels, and contamination. State run administrations likewise are worried about the control of pestilence and pandemic illnesses, laying out rules for fitting clinical reactions and separation methods, and giving travel alerts to keep the spread of sickness from impacted regions.

Different general wellbeing offices have been laid out to help control and screen illness inside social orders, on both public and worldwide levels. For instance, the Unified Realm's General Wellbeing Demonstration of 1848 laid out an exceptional general wellbeing service for Britain and Ribs. In the US, general wellbeing is considered and facilitated on a public level by the Communities for Infectious prevention and Counteraction (CDC). Globally, the World Wellbeing Association (WHO) assumes a comparable part. WHO is particularly significant in giving help to the execution of hierarchical and authoritative techniques for taking care of issues related with wellbeing and sickness in less-created nations around the world? Inside these nations, medical conditions, limits of assets, training of wellbeing staff, and different variables should be considered in planning wellbeing administration frameworks.

Progresses in science and medication in created nations, including the age of immunizations and anti-microbial, have been major in carrying imperative guide to nations beset by a high weight of sickness. However, in spite of the development of assets and enhancements in the activation of these assets to the most seriously distressed regions, the frequency of preventable sickness and of ignored tropical illness remains uncommonly high around the world. Lessening the effect and commonness of these sicknesses is a significant objective of worldwide general wellbeing. The steadiness of such illnesses on the planet, nonetheless, fills in as a significant sign of the challenges that wellbeing associations and social orders keep on going up against.

History of general wellbeing

A survey of the verifiable improvement of general wellbeing, which started in old times, underscores how different general wellbeing ideas have developed. Authentic general wellbeing estimates remembered quarantine of infection casualties for the medieval times and endeavors to further develop disinfection following the fourteenth century plague pandemics. Populace expansions in Europe carried with them expanded consciousness of baby passing's and a multiplication of clinics. These advancements thus prompted the foundation of current general wellbeing organizations and associations, intended to control sickness inside networks and to direct the accessibility and circulation of prescriptions.

The majority of the world's old people groups rehearsed tidiness and individual cleanliness, frequently for strict reasons, including, clearly, a wish to be unadulterated according to their divine beings. The Book of scriptures, for instance, has numerous requests and restrictions about spotless and messy living. Religion, regulation, and specially were inseparably entwined. For millennia social orders viewed pandemics as heavenly decisions on the fiendishness of humanity. The possibility that plague is because of normal causes, like environment and actual climate, in any case, bit by bit created. This extraordinary development in thought occurred in Greece during the fifth and fourth hundreds of years BCE and addressed the principal endeavor at a levelheaded, logical hypothesis of sickness causation. A relationship among intestinal sickness and marshes, for instance, was laid out mid (503-403 BCE), despite the fact that the explanations behind the affiliation were dark. In the book Airs, Waters, and Places, remembered to have been composed by Greek doctor Hippocrates in the fifth or fourth century BCE, the primary methodical endeavor was made to present a causal connection between human illnesses and the climate. Until the new studies of bacteriology and immunology arose into the nineteenth 100 years, this book gave a hypothetical premise to the understanding of endemic illness (that persevering in a specific territory) and pandemic sickness (that influencing various individuals inside a somewhat brief period).

Current authoritative and regulatory examples

Worldwide associations

Since antiquated times, the spread of scourge sickness exhibited the requirement for worldwide collaboration for wellbeing security. Early endeavors toward worldwide control of illness showed up in public isolations in Europe and the Center East. The primary proper global wellbeing meeting, held in Paris in 1851, was trailed by a progression of comparable gatherings pointed toward drafting worldwide quarantine guidelines. A long-lasting wellbeing association, the Global Office of General Wellbeing (Office Worldwide hygiene Publique), was laid out in Paris in 1907 to get warning of serious transferable illnesses from partaking nations, to send this data to the part nations, and to study and foster clean shows and quarantine guidelines on transportation and train travel. This association was eventually consumed by the World Wellbeing Association (WHO) in 1948.

In the Americas, the association of worldwide wellbeing most likely started with a provincial wellbeing meeting in Rio de Janeiro in 1887. From 1889 forward there were a few meetings of American nations, which drove eventually to the foundation of the Container American Sterile Department, which was made a territorial office of WHO in 1949, when it became known as the Skillet American Wellbeing Association.

The ascent and decline of wellbeing associations has been impacted by wars and their aftermaths. After The Second Great War a Wellbeing Segment of the Class of Countries was laid out (1923) and worked until The Second Great War. After the conflict, the Unified Countries Help and Restoration Organization (UNRRA) was set up; it handled dislodged people so as to forestall the spread of illness. It was liable for the arranging steps that prompted the foundation of WHO as a unique organization of the Unified Countries. WHO is worried about physical, mental, and social prosperity and not simply with the shortfall of sickness?

Crafted by WHO is completed under the heading of the World Wellbeing Get together, which has delegates from the part states. The main gathering gave thought to illnesses and issues that exist in huge region of the world and that loan themselves to global activity. Intestinal sickness, tuberculosis, physically sent illness, the advancement of wellbeing; ecological circumstances liable for a huge extent of passing's, and sustenance were given need. Different areas of need have been incorporated since.

Among significant elements of the association are the warning administrations proposed to states through its provincial staff. Provincial workplaces in various nations, both industrialized and less-created, as well as nearby delegates in some less-created nations, assist WHO with keeping in touch with requirements and wellsprings of monetary guide. In particular fields, various master panels think about unambiguous inquiries.

WHO keeps up with cozy associations with other Joined Countries offices, especially the Unified Countries Kids' Asset (UNICEF) and the Food and Agribusiness Association (FAO), and with worldwide work associations. From its origin in 1946, UNICEF zeroed in its guide on maternal and kid wellbeing administrations and the control of diseases, particularly in youngsters. Need has been given to the development of immunizations, the organization of natural disinfection, the arrangement of clean water, and the preparation of neighborhood faculty in their own nations (particularly in country regions). Help is diverted through coordinated wellbeing administrations in less-created nations. Late endeavors have focused on convincing legislatures to attempt public overviews to recognize the essential necessities of their youngsters and to devise fitting public approaches.

Crafted by WHO incorporates three primary classes of exercises. In the first place, it is a clearinghouse for data about sickness all through the world, and it has fostered a uniform framework for revealing illnesses and reasons for death. It has laid out globally acknowledged principles for drugs and drawn up a rundown of "fundamental" (viable, modest, and dependable) drugs. It has supported and funded many examination projects all through the world. Second, WHO has elevated mass missions to control pestilence and endemic infections, a significant number of which have been very effective? Third, WHO endeavors to fortify and extend the general wellbeing organization and administrations of part nations by giving specialized counsel, groups of specialists to do reviews and show tasks, and help on the side of local and public wellbeing advancement projects?

Created nations

Techniques for wellbeing organization differ from one country to another. Significant wellbeing capabilities are as often as possible gathered in an office that is liable for wellbeing and for related capabilities. In the Assembled Realm they are completed by the Division of Wellbeing and Government backed retirement; in the US the Branch of Wellbeing and Human Administrations controls the projects covered by public regulation.

Not many focal divisions of wellbeing are sweeping; different offices likewise work clinical projects or some likeness thereof. No nation puts the wellbeing administrations of its tactical powers under the focal wellbeing organization. Since solidarity of control at the middle is unreasonable, coordination is significant. Focal organization is additionally confounded in government frameworks. In the US there are 50 expresses, no two of which have similar examples of wellbeing association.

Designs divided between created nations

The authority liable for the organization of public wellbeing undertakings is as a rule an individual from the bureau. Warning chambers are much of the time used to bring the thoughts of driving researchers, wellbeing specialists, and local area pioneers to bear on significant public medical conditions.

An association that gives fundamental local area wellbeing administrations under the heading of a clinical official is known as a neighborhood wellbeing unit. It is generally represented by a neighborhood authority. Its projects might incorporate maternal and youngster wellbeing, transmittable infectious prevention, natural disinfection, support of records for factual purposes, wellbeing training of general society, general wellbeing nursing, clinical consideration, and, frequently, school wellbeing administrations. The nearby wellbeing unit can give the managerial system to a more extensive scope of local area wellbeing administrations, including the consideration of the matured, of the truly incapacitated, and of the constantly sick and emotional well-being administrations. Albeit social government assistance administrations might be given by a different office, there are benefits in amalgamating wellbeing and government assistance administrations, in light of the fact that a family's wellbeing and social issues will generally be interrelated.

The populace served by a neighborhood wellbeing unit might be two or three thousand or a few hundred thousand. There are considerably various issues engaged with overseeing wellbeing administrations for a huge rustic region that is meagerly populated and a district with a populace of a couple of million. One issue of directing nearby wellbeing administrations is whether or not they ought to be controlled by free neighborhood specialists or coordinated territorially to guarantee coordination and successful reference and to stay away from duplication of administrations.

Clinical consideration is offered as a public support somewhat in many nations. It could be restricted to the hospitalization of people distressed with specific infirmities — for instance, mental sickness, tuberculosis, ongoing ailment, and intense diseases. Exhaustive wellbeing administrations might be accommodated some particular populace gatherings, as in Canada and the US, where the central government gives care to Indians and Eskimos. Numerous nations have necessary clinical protection, and some consolidate the socialization of clinics with clinical protection covering general clinical consideration, as in Denmark. Full-scale socialization of wellbeing administrations exists in a couple of nations, including the Unified Realm and New Zealand. Such associated wellbeing administrations are frequently on the other hand portrayed as frameworks of public, or general, medical services.

In nations like the Netherlands and the US, where deliberate and charitable associations support an impressive portion of the wellbeing administrations and work the vast majority of the overall medical clinics, there is pluralism in wellbeing organization. This makes coordination troublesome, yet willful exertion enjoys the benefits of including residents straightforwardly in the improvement of wellbeing administrations and of advancing trial and error in organization.

There is a pattern toward territorial preparation of thorough wellbeing administrations for characterized populaces. In an admired arrangement, the principal level of contact between the populace and the framework, which can be called essential consideration, is given by wellbeing faculty who work in local area wellbeing focuses and who arrive at past the wellbeing habitats into the networks and homes with preventive, primitive, and instructive administrations. At a higher degree of care, experts in local area clinics give optional consideration to patients alluded from the essential consideration places. At last, tertiary, or super specialty, care is given by a significant clinical focus. The different levels of this provincial plan are connected by a two-way progression of clinical records, patients, and wellbeing staff. Regionalization has been most completely accomplished in Europe and least so in North America, where willful clinics give the majority of the momentary general administrations and hold independence in their organization.

Varieties among created nations

Among the created nations, there is significant variety in the association and organization of wellbeing administrations. The Unified Realm, for instance, has a Public Wellbeing Administration with significant independence given to neighborhood government for execution. The US has a pluralistic way to deal with wellbeing administrations, in which nearby, state, and public legislatures have fluctuating areas of obligation, with the confidential area assuming a conspicuous part.

During the principal half of the twentieth 100 years in the Unified Realm, the accentuation moved progressively from natural toward individual general wellbeing. A progression of rules, of which the Maternity and Youngster Government assistance Act (1918) was presumably the main, put liability regarding a large portion of the work on district states. Public health care coverage (1911) gave advantages to 16 million laborers and denoted the start of an interaction whereupon the Public Wellbeing Administration Act (1946) was fabricated.

The Public Wellbeing Administration Act gave extensive inclusion to the vast majority of the wellbeing administrations, including medical clinics, general practice, and general wellbeing. The help stayed at the fringe, be that as it may, in three kinds of care:

(1) Essential clinical consideration is given by family doctors or general professionals. This assistance is coordinated locally by a chief committee. Each broad specialist is liable for giving essential consideration to a gathering on a specific library.

(2) Expert meeting and short term and ongoing treatment are given in emergency clinics under the bearing of territorial specialists. A later idea makes each locale general clinic liable for giving emergency clinic administrations to a characterized populace.

(3) Administrations, for example, wellbeing visiting, home nursing, home aides, domiciliary maternity care, the counteraction of disease, and the arrangement of

wellbeing focuses are the obligation of nearby specialists. In the Soviet Association the assurance and advancement of general wellbeing was the obligation of the state. There was free community to all types of clinical consideration. The standards of the wellbeing administrations were finished coordination of remedial and preventive administrations, medication as a social help, preventive projects, wellbeing focuses or polyclinics (centers in which various illnesses were taken care of), and local area support.

The general wellbeing administrations for the Soviet Association were coordinated by the Service of Wellbeing. Every one of 15 republics of the association had its own service. Every republic was partitioned into oblast (territories), which thus were isolated into rayon (regions) lastly into uchastoki (areas). Every development had its own wellbeing office responsible to the following most elevated division.

There were deeply grounded reference strategies, from the polyclinics and more modest emergency clinics in the uchastoki to the bigger rayon emergency clinics, and from Felds hers (paramedical faculty prepared in clinical consideration) and other paramedical staff to internists and pediatricians and, when vital, to all the more profoundly concentrated work force.

The wellbeing administrations of the US can be considered at three levels: neighborhood, state, and government.

Locally, in urban areas or provinces, there is significant independence inside wide rules created by the state. The size and extent of nearby projects fluctuate, however a portion of their capabilities are control of transmittable sicknesses; facilities for moms and youngsters, especially for specific preventive and indicative administrations; general wellbeing nursing administrations; natural wellbeing administrations; wellbeing training; essential insights; local area wellbeing focuses, clinics, and other clinical consideration offices; local area wellbeing arranging and coordination.

At the state level, a division of wellbeing is accused of generally speaking liability regarding wellbeing; however various organizations may really be involved.

The state branch of wellbeing normally has five capabilities: general wellbeing and preventive projects; clinical and custodial consideration like the activity of medical clinics for dysfunctional behavior; development and improvement of clinics, clinical offices, and wellbeing focuses; licensure for wellbeing reasons for people, organizations, and endeavors serving general society; and monetary and specialized help to neighborhood legislatures for directing wellbeing programs.

At the government, or public, level, the General Wellbeing Administration of the Division of Wellbeing and Human Administrations is the vital wellbeing organization, yet a few different offices have wellbeing interests and obligations. Government wellbeing offices acknowledge liability regarding further developing state and nearby administrations, for controlling highway wellbeing dangers, and for working with different nations on worldwide wellbeing matters. The central government likewise has the accompanying explicit obligations:

(1) Shielding the US from transferable sicknesses from abroad,

(2) Accommodating the clinical requirements of military work force, veterans, vendor sailors, and Native Americans,

(3) Safeguarding shoppers against unclean or misbranded food varieties, medications, and beauty care products, and

(4) Managing creation of natural items, like antibodies. Furthermore, the central government advances and supports clinical examination, wellbeing administrations, and instructive projects all through the country.

Willful exertion is a huge piece of wellbeing work in the US. Willful organizations in the wellbeing field capability generally at the neighborhood level, however they additionally might be dynamic at state and public levels. Upheld to a great extent through confidential sources, these offices add to programs connected with instruction, examination, and wellbeing administrations.

Clinical consideration is given and paid to through many channels, including public establishments, for example, metropolitan, province, state, and government wellbeing focuses, medical clinics, and clinical consideration programs, and through confidential emergency clinics and confidential experts working either alone or, progressively, in gatherings. By and large, clinical consideration is supported by open assets, deliberate health care coverage, or individual installment.

In this manner, in the US there is extraordinary assortment in the substance, degree, and nature of wellbeing administrations. These administrations are given by a few free offices. Essentially, in any case, they comprise a functioning organization for the security and advancement of human wellbeing.

There is mindfulness that, while the current arrangement of wellbeing administrations gives excellent consideration to many, there are others for whom the consideration is either missing or unacceptable; this has added to changes in the direction of wellbeing administrations in the US. In like manner, steeply increasing expenses of clinical consideration prompted reevaluation of the whole arrangement of individual clinical consideration and proposition for new frameworks of giving and supporting medical care.

Non-industrial nations

Emerging nations have once in a while been impacted in their ways to deal with medical care issues by the created nations that have played a part in their set of experiences. For instance, the nations in Africa and Asia that were once states of England have instructive projects and medical care frameworks that reflect English examples; however there have been variations to neighborhood needs. Comparative impacts might be seen in nations affected by France, the Netherlands, and Belgium.

In any case, while clear examples in medical care association can be found among a few less-created nations, there likewise exist wide varieties and holes in the wellbeing assets and organization tracked down in other less-created nations. These varieties and holes are more articulated in less-created versus created locales on the grounds that inside the previous are mind boggling factors (like political or cultural flimsiness) equipped for confusing and some of the time even completely upsetting the organization of medical care. Nations with such unsteady medical care framework frequently are subject to help from global associations.

In spite of varieties from one country to another, a typical, in the event that to some degree romanticized, managerial example might be drawn for less-created nations. All wellbeing administrations, with the exception of a limited quantity of private practice, are under a service of wellbeing, in which there are around five agencies, or divisions — clinic administrations, wellbeing administrations, schooling and preparing, work force, and exploration and arranging. Clinic and wellbeing administrations are appropriated all through the country. At the fringe of the framework are dispensaries, or wellbeing stations, frequently set up by a couple of people with restricted preparing? The dispensaries are frequently of restricted viability and are moved up to full wellbeing communities whenever the situation allows. Wellbeing focuses and their exercises are the underpinning of the framework. Wellbeing focuses are normally staffed by assistants who have four to 10 years of fundamental schooling in addition to one to four years of specialized preparing. The staff might incorporate a maternity specialist, helper nurture, a sanitarian, and a clinical partner. The collaborators, prepared in the determination and therapy of disorder, allude to a doctor the issues that are past their own skill. Together, these helpers give complete consideration to a populace of 10,000 to 25,000. A few wellbeing communities along with a region emergency clinic serve a locale of around 100,000 to 200,000 individuals. All wellbeing administrations are under the obligation of the region clinical official, who, helped by other expert and helper staff, coordinates the wellbeing endeavors into an extensive program.

Of focal significance is the dispersion of obligations among assistants and experts. The helpers, by taking care of the enormous number of generally basic issues, permit the experts to care for just the more perplexing issues, to oversee and show the assistants, and to design and deal with the projects.

The locale emergency clinic is reliant upon a provincial clinic, to which patients with complex issues can be alluded for more-particular administrations.

Regulatory heading of both local wellbeing administrations and provincial emergency clinic administrations can be joined at this level under a territorial clinical official. The focal organization of the service of wellbeing gives strategies and direction to a whole wellbeing administration and, in certain cases, likewise gives a focal arranging unit.

Issues of transportation and correspondence over significant stretches, deficiencies of staff and different assets, and deficiencies in staff arrangement and inspiration frequently lead to breakdowns in the framework. Regardless, the general wellbeing administrations created in African and Asian nations have commonly given a sound premise to future improvement inside the structure of public turn of events.

The association of general wellbeing administrations in Latin American nations contrasts considerably from those of Africa and Asia. These distinctions are a declaration of the different verifiable foundations of the districts. The Latin American nations are by and large more well-to-do than those of Asia and Africa. Confidential practice is more inescapable and private or willful offices are more unmistakable. Wellbeing administrations are given to a great extent by nearby and public legislatures. Numerous Latin American nations additionally have frameworks of centers and medical clinics for laborers supported by managers and laborers. The dissemination of wellbeing administrations, with wellbeing focuses, clinics, and preventive administrations, is generally like Africa and Asia. The Latin American nations, nonetheless, have utilized assistant's not exactly African and Asian nations. Latin America has spearheaded in the improvement of wellbeing arranging techniques. Chile has one of the most-developed ways to deal with wellbeing arranging on the planet.

Thailand was rarely colonized and hence has no authentic impact inclining toward a specific example of wellbeing administrations. The Thai Service of Wellbeing has an advanced arrangement of clinics and wellbeing focuses the nation over to serve both provincial and metropolitan individuals. In 2001 the nation took on a subsidized medical coverage plan, upheld by and large by government supporting and enhanced by confidential assets. Inside the general wellbeing administrations of Thailand, there are various separate divisions — e.g., for tuberculosis, physically sent illnesses, and sustenance.

Medical issues and impediments

The troubles of giving wellbeing administrations to individuals of the less-created nations include a group of interrelated issues. These emerge from the idea of the illnesses and risks to wellbeing, lacking and maldistributed assets, the plan of wellbeing administration frameworks, and the training of wellbeing staff in those frameworks. Woven through the wellbeing projects of the less-created nations and muddling them at both family and public levels are the tensions related with quickly developing populaces.

There are contrasts not just in that frame of mind of sicknesses of various nations yet in addition in the rates at which they happen and in the age bunches included. Future in certain nations is not exactly a portion of that in others, basically due to high passing rates among little kids in the less-created nations. In Southeast Asia, for instance, kids under age five are somewhere in the range of three and multiple times bound to kick the bucket than offspring of a similar age bunch in the Americas. The baby (under one year old enough) death rate in Africa is multiple times that in Europe, and the demise rate in kids under age five (under-five death rate) is in excess of multiple times more noteworthy.

The chief reasons for ailment and demise among little kids in the less-created world are looseness of the bowels, respiratory diseases, and hunger, which are all personally connected with culture, custom, and financial status. Unhealthiness might result from food customs when restrictions and straightforward oversight lead to hardship of youngsters. Gastroenteritis (aggravation of the covering of the stomach and digestion tracts, for the most part with going with loose bowels) and respiratory diseases are frequently because of irresistible organic entities, some of which might be impervious to antimicrobial medications. The interrelationships of these illnesses increment the intricacy of treating them. Unhealthiness is much of the time the basic guilty party. In addition to the fact that it causes harm itself, like impediment of physical and mental turn of events, yet it likewise appears to make way for different diseases. A malnourished kid creates gastroenteritis, failure to eat, further shortcoming, and afterward parchedness. The debilitated kid is helpless to a deadly disease, like pneumonia. Or on the other hand, to finish the endless loop, contamination can influence protein digestion in manners that add to hunger.

Another variable that adds to this is family size. Lack of healthy sustenance, with related passing and handicap, happens most frequently in youngsters naturally introduced to huge and ineffectively dispersed families. The subsequent high passing rate among little youngsters frequently supports the propensity of guardians to have more kids. Individuals are not leaned to restrict the size of their families until it is evident that their kids have a sensible opportunity of endurance. Subsequently, there is a richness mortality cycle in which high fruitfulness, reflected in enormous quantities of little youngsters jammed into an unfortunate home, prompts high youth mortality, which thus empowers high ripeness. This is the premise of the conviction that populace control projects ought to incorporate compelling method for lessening pointless passing's among youngsters.

Among limits of assets, deficiencies of prepared faculty are among the most significant. Proportions of populace to doctors, medical caretakers, and beds give a sign of the reality of these lacks and furthermore of the incredible contrasts from one country to another. Accordingly, the extent of populace to doctors in less-created nations fluctuates definitely. Cash is a critical figure medical service: it decides the number of wellbeing staff can be prepared, the number of can be kept up with in the field, and the assets that they should work with when they are there. Administrative consumptions on medical care change extraordinarily from one country to another.

In the endeavor to give medical services to its kin, a nation should have sufficient assets set up to manage critical and complex issues, for example, obstetric and careful crises for which emergency clinic care is fundamental. Simultaneously, it should likewise effectively venture into the networks and homes to track down the individuals who need care however don't look for it and should find the reasons for such sicknesses as unhealthiness and gastroenteritis.

Instruction of wellbeing faculty

In the training of wellbeing faculty, a specific arrangement of issues arises. Instructive projects for helpers are fit to the neighborhood circumstance, maybe in light of the fact that they were not laid out in the more-created nations. Clinical and nursing training, then again, is like that of the further developed nations, and it plans understudies better for working in industrialized nations than in their own. This nonconformist among instruction and the tasks to be done has likely contributed significantly both to the incapability of wellbeing administration frameworks and to the movement of expert faculty to the more-created nations.

Progress in general wellbeing

Among the more-created nations the accompanying patterns are evident.

Expanding interest of public state run administrations

Previously, state run administrations were mostly worried about essential medical conditions, like ecological disinfection, clinical consideration of poor people, quarantine, and the control of transferable sicknesses. Progressively, many have expanded their exercises into the field of clinical consideration administrations in the home, facility, and clinic, in order to give complete medical care to whole networks. Three elements have impacted this pattern: (1) inflated expenses of clinical consideration, (2) expanded enthusiasm for the financial misfortune to a country from disorder, and (3) uplifted public interest in friendly administrations. In numerous locales, wellbeing and social government assistance are perceived as correlative, and social regulation will in general cover both, empowering close collaboration among wellbeing and social government assistance administrations.

Changing ideas of preventable infection

Previously, the term preventable illness alluded to a delineated gathering of irresistible infections. The term has gained a more extensive importance, in any case, since numerous normal noninfectious sicknesses are preventable too. In the cutting edge time, preventive wellbeing administrations manage an extensive variety of wellbeing dangers, like harmful cancers, stiffness, cardiovascular sicknesses, other persistent and degenerative illnesses, and even mishaps.

Joining of preventive and clinical consideration administrations

Clinical consideration had its starting point in the philanthropic thought process of really focusing on the wiped out, while preventive wellbeing administrations sprang from the need to shield a sound climate from pestilence sicknesses. They developed separated, yet the pattern became to coordinate them inside a far reaching wellbeing administration. Such coordination was the central rule of general wellbeing in the Soviet

Association, wherein all nearby wellbeing administrations were focused in the locale medical clinic under one organization. Today, in European nations and somewhere else, particularly in provincial regions, the two branches are united by the neighborhood clinical specialist.

Arrangements coordinated toward better emotional well-being

Emotional wellness has a spot in the preventive administrations. Upgrades in game plans for psychological wellness incorporate the arrangement of short term facilities and ongoing facilities at general clinics for early crackpots, an expansion in kid direction and marriage-direction centers, and plans for the consideration of drunkards and medication fiends. There have additionally been critical improvements in the treatment of maladjusted citizenry. Gains in comprehension of psychoneuroses by broad specialists and the improvement of examination offices are additionally important.

Developing accentuation on wellbeing instruction

Numerous nations have extended their obligation to wellbeing schooling, as a rule in collaboration with deliberate organizations. The best work is done at the neighborhood level, particularly in schools. The pattern has been toward an extension of wellbeing schooling as a fundamental preventive wellbeing administration.

The biostatistician, epidemiological methodology

A factual help is fundamental in arranging, controlling, and assessing wellbeing administrations. The interest of public experts in clinical consideration plans has expanded the significance of measurements on the rate of illnesses and different issues, as well as the study of disease transmission important to battle them. Both are crucial in the preparation, association, and assessment of clinical consideration plans. Generally, the epidemiological technique was utilized for irresistible sicknesses; however it has been utilized progressively for noninfectious infections and the issues of clinical consideration.

Changes coming about because of a maturing populace

In more-well-off nations, an expansion in more seasoned age bunches achieves the requirement for general wellbeing offices to offer unique types of assistance for them. Medical care of the older incorporates measures to forestall untimely maturing and ongoing and degenerative infections and to face the mental issues coming about because of dejection and dormancy. In the 21st century the rising pervasiveness of dementia in older populaces presented huge difficulties for general wellbeing. Geriatric centers and helped living offices have been gotten up positioned address these issues and to direct investigation into the course of senescence.

A developing populace requires an expansion in modern and business exercises, which add to the volume of contaminations that undermine the climate, streams, lakes, and seas and horrendously affect regular biology. These impacts can cause decreases in air and water quality and in species that are wellsprings of food sources and drugs, all of which can have ramifications for human wellbeing.

Numerous nations have moved toward the control of ecological decay, and method for worldwide guideline have likewise been proposed and, in certain cases, executed.

Considering the enormous quantities of serious medical issues confronting individuals in less-created nations and the restricted assets for managing those issues, significant advancement likewise frequently accompanies some level of stagnation or even relapse.

Irresistible infectious prevention

Measles and polio are instances of transferable infections that have been brought under close control all through the world. Smallpox, when a feared irresistible illness of youngsters, was formally proclaimed killed in 1980. For different sicknesses, for example, cholera and meningitis, there has been significant development in understanding that might add to their possible control. Similarly, more prominent admittance to medicate treatments and counteraction mindfulness in the mid-21st century added to a decrease in new instances of Helps (AIDS) and a decrease in passings from Helps, a sickness that had first been distinguished in 1981. Certain parasitic illnesses spread as individuals achieved changes in their current circumstance; the expansion in schistosomiasis (pervasion with blood accident through snails as the middle hosts) in water system and human-made lake regions is a model. Research shed light on recently arising mosquito-borne illnesses, like Zika fever and chikungunya fever, as well as on methods of transmission and method for forestalling the spread of profoundly infectious sicknesses like Ebola.

Broad hunger, especially protein-calorie lack of healthy sustenance in little youngsters, stays an issue. Protein-rich food enhancements and more viable instructive projects are pointed toward combatting under nutrition and ailing health in less-created nations.

Family wellbeing

The issues of quickly developing populaces have significant outcomes at both the family and the public level. Issues of maternal and youngster wellbeing, human propagation, and human hereditary qualities are parts of the more noteworthy issue of the strength of the entire family as a solitary and principal social unit. As needs be, family wellbeing, including family arranging, is a significant part of general wellbeing administrations.

Wellbeing faculty

There is far and wide acknowledgment of deficiencies in both number and training of wellbeing work force. The pattern is toward organizing the schooling of wellbeing staff with the specific wellbeing administration wherein they will work. This pattern requires cozy connections between instructive organizations and the offices answerable for wellbeing administrations.

The mix of corrective and preventive administrations in extensive wellbeing hierarchical examples assumes a significant part in local area wellbeing. Wellbeing advancement, sickness anticipation, and the relieving and restoration of the evil are united into one organization of incorporated administrations that ranges to the local area level.

Public wellbeing arranging

Complex navigation is engaged with designating restricted wellbeing administration assets to enormous quantities of individuals, a cycle that underscores the job of wellbeing arranging and that requires successful wellbeing administration frameworks. Various nations have laid out wellbeing arranging units in the service of wellbeing or the public arranging association. A significant part of public wellbeing arranging is the nearby coordination between arranging, planning, carrying out, and assessing programs.

Policy implementation

Policy implementation, the execution of government arrangements. Today policy implementation is frequently viewed as including additionally some obligation regarding deciding the strategies and projects of states. In particular, it is the preparation, sorting out, coordinating, planning, and controlling of government activities.

Policy implementation is a component, everything being equal, whatever their arrangement of government. Inside countries policy management is drilled at the focal, moderate, and neighborhood levels. To be sure, the connections between various degrees of government inside a solitary country comprise a developing issue of policy implementation.

In the vast majority of the world the foundation of exceptionally prepared regulatory, leader, or mandate classes has made policy implementation a particular calling. The group of public executives is normally called the common assistance. In the US, the elitist class meanings generally connected to the common help was deliberately deserted or from the mid-twentieth hundred years, with the outcome that government employees were perceived as experts and esteemed for their ability.

Generally the common help is diverged from different bodies serving the state full time, like the military, the legal executive, and the police. Particular administrations, in some cases alluded to as logical or proficient common administrations, give specialized as opposed to general managerial help. Customarily, in many nations, a qualification is likewise made between the home common help and those people connected abroad on conciliatory obligations. A government worker, in this manner, is one of a collection of people who are straightforwardly utilized in the organization of the interior undertakings of the state and whose job and status are not political, pastoral, military, or constabulary.

In many nations the common help does exclude nearby government or public enterprises. In certain nations, but — especially those unitary states where common organization is essential for the focal government — a few commonplace staffs are government employees. In the, all of us levels of government have their own common administrations

— bureaucratic, state, and nearby — and a common help is explicitly that piece of legislative help entered by assessment and offering super durable residency.

Certain qualities are normal to all thoughtful administrations. Senior government employees are viewed as the expert consultants to the people who form state strategy. In certain nations section necessities for a vocation in the higher common help pressure capabilities in specialized fields like bookkeeping, financial matters, medication, and designing. In different nations legitimate preparation is considered proper, and in others no particular specialized or scholastic discipline is expected among contender for senior posts. Anything their exact capabilities, senior government employees are proficient as they would say of public undertakings is remembered to give them the information on the cutoff points inside which state strategy can be made powerful and of the plausible managerial aftereffects of various blueprints. Government employees in each nation are supposed to exhort, caution, and help those answerable for state strategy and, when this has been chosen, to give the association to carrying out it. The obligation regarding strategy choices lies with the political individuals from the chief (those individuals who have been chosen or designated to provide political guidance to government and, usually, vocation government workers). Generally, government employees are safeguarded from public fault or blame for their recommendation. The demonstrations of their organization may, in any case, be dependent upon extraordinary legal controls from which no individual from the leader can safeguard them.

Common administrations are coordinated upon standard progressive lines, in which an order structure rises pyramid-style from the most minimal workplaces to the most noteworthy. This order suggests compliance to the legal orders of a prevalent, and to keep up with this framework the progressive system of workplaces is set apart by fixed positions, with distinct obligations, explicit powers, and pay rates and honors dispassionately evaluated. In a nations there might be immediate arrangement to higher office of people not recently utilized by the help, but rather and still, at the end of the day a perceived arrangement of inner advancement underscores the idea of the progressive pyramid.

This article talks about the development of policy implementation through history as well as its advancement under various political frameworks. Unique consideration is paid to the issues of managerial regulation and administrative construction. For conversation of a subject vital to policy implementation, see government financial strategy. For additional conversation of the different systems under which policy implementation works, see political framework.

Policy management has old starting points. In days of yore the Egyptians and Greeks coordinated public undertakings by office, and the essential officeholders were viewed as being basically answerable for overseeing equity, keeping up with the rule of law, and giving bounty. The Romans fostered a more modern framework under their domain, making particular managerial orders for equity, military issues, money and tax collection, international concerns, and inward issues, each with its own chief officials of state. An intricate regulatory design, later imitated by the Roman Catholic Church, covered the whole domain, with an order of officials revealing back through their bosses to the head. This complex construction vanished after the fall of the Western Roman Domain in the fifth hundred years, yet a significant number of its practices gone on in the Byzantine Realm in the east, where common help rule was reflected in the derogatory utilization of the word Byzantines'.

Early European regulatory designs created from the illustrious families of the archaic period. For the rest of the twelfth century official obligations inside the imperial families were not well characterized, every now and again with different holders of a similar post. Exemptions were the better-characterized places of head servant (liable for the arrangement of wine), steward (answerable for devouring game plans), chamberlain (frequently accused of getting and paying out cash kept in the imperial dozing chamber), and chancellor (normally a minister with responsibilities regarding composing and applying the seal in the ruler's name). With the thirteenth century a partition started between the simply homegrown elements of the regal family and the capabilities associated with overseeing the state. The more seasoned family presents tended on vanishes, become sinecures, or decrease in significance. The workplace of chancellor, which had forever been worried about issues of state, made due to turn into the main connection between the old court workplaces and present day services, and the improvement of the cutting edge depository or fund service can be followed back to the chamberlain's office in the illustrious family.

From the center of the thirteenth century three organizations started to arise as the significant bodies for taking care of issues of express: the high court (advancing fundamentally from the chancellery), the exchequer, and the collegial regal chamber. In Britain and France, in any case, it was only after the mid-fourteenth century that such bodies arose. In Brandenburg, which was represented by a balloter (a sovereign with an option to choose the Blessed Roman ruler) and which later shaped the premise of the Prussian state, they became unmistakable elements just toward the start of the seventeenth hundred years.

Aside from equity and depository divisions, which started in old court workplaces, current ecclesiastical designs in Europe created out of the imperial committees, which were strong assemblages of aristocrats delegated by the ruler. From the division of work inside these body the rulers' secretaries, at first given low status inside a committee, arose as maybe the principal proficient government employees in Europe in the cutting edge sense. The closeness of the secretaries to the ruler gave them more information on imperial aims, and their general lastingness gave them more noteworthy skill specifically matters of state than could be found among the more transient aristocrats on the chamber. They were additionally helped by staffs. The secretaries filled in significance in the fifteenth and sixteenth hundreds of years as they turned out to be pretty much full individuals from the chamber.

The dispersion of capabilities among secretaries was at first in view of topography. In Britain this topographical portion — with, for instance, a secretary of the North and a secretary of the South — continued until 1782, when the workplaces of home and unfamiliar secretary were made. In France a more perplexing distribution of regional obligations among secretaries of state had started to give way to useful obligations toward the finish of the ancien régime in 1789.

The common help in China was without a doubt the longest enduring ever; it was first coordinated, alongside a brought together organization, during the Han line (206 BCE-220 CE) and worked on under the Tang (618-907) and sung (960-1279). The organization was coordinated well to such an extent that the example remained until 1912. During the Sung line there fostered the full utilization of common help assessments. Competitors were exposed to progressive disposal through composed tests on three levels, in excess of 100 people starting the trial for everyone who arose fruitful. Despite the fact that there was solid accentuation on the Chinese Works of art (since information on the Works of art was remembered to frame the ideals of a productive member of society), there was likewise a work to devise level headed and significant tests for functional characteristics, and there were in every case long conflicts over topic and testing strategies. To safeguard the obscurity of the up-and-comer and to guarantee decency in reviewing, assessment papers were duplicated by representatives, examinees were recognized by number just, and three analysts read each paper. Higher authorities were special to select junior family members for admission to the organization, yet the extraordinary weight on assessment grades in advancement, the utilization of yearly legitimacy evaluations, and the act of enrolling many lower authorities from the positions of the administrative help guaranteed a significant opportunity of chance.

The groundwork's of present day policy implementation in Europe were laid in Prussia in the late seventeenth and eighteenth hundreds of years. The balloters of Brandenburg (who from 1701 were the rulers of Prussia) considered an inflexibly unified government a method for guaranteeing security and promoting dynastic goals. Their primary exertion was dedicated in the main occurrence to the concealment of the independence of the urban communities and to the disposal of the primitive honors of the gentry. Government employees were thusly designated by the focal government to oversee the regions, where the administration of crown lands and the association of the tactical framework were consolidated in a Krieg's-und-Dominion-hammer ("Office of War and

Crown Grounds"). Subordinate to these workplaces were the Stearate ("charge councilors"), who controlled the organization of the districts and cooperatives. These authorities were undeniably designated by the focal government and were mindful to it. At the peak of the new apparatus of government was the sovereign.

This brought together framework was fortified by making an extraordinary corps of government employees. In the first place these government workers — from genuine perspective workers of the crown — were conveyed from Berlin to manage such simply military matters as enlisting, billeting, and victualing the soldiers, yet over time they stretched out their management to common matters too. By 1713 there were obviously conspicuous authoritative units managing in common undertakings and staffed by crown government employees.

Exceptional mandates in 1722 and 1748 controlled enlistment to the common help. Senior authorities were expected to propose to the lord the names of applicants appropriate for arrangement to the higher posts, while the aide general proposed noncommissioned officials reasonable for subordinate regulatory posts. Further advances were required all through the eighteenth hundred years to regularize the arrangement of enrollment, advancement, and inside association. These issues were united in a solitary General Code declared in 1794. The legitimacy arrangement of arrangement covered a wide range of posts, and the overall guideline set down was that "exceptional regulations and directions decide the delegating power to various common help rank, their capabilities, and the fundamental assessments expected from various branches and various positions." Passage to the higher common help required a college degree in cameralistics, which, however stringently talking the study of public money, included likewise the investigation of regulatory regulation, police organization, bequest the board, and rural financial matters. After the degree course, contender for the higher common help spent a further time of regulated useful preparation in different parts of the organization, toward the finish of which they went through a further oral and composed assessment. The fundamental standards of current common administrations are to be tracked down in this Broad Code.

A key change in the situation with the government employee occurred because of the French Transformation of 1789. The fall of the ancien régime and the making of a republic implied that the government employee was viewed as the worker presently not of the lord yet rather of the state — despite the fact that standard by a ruler or sovereign was before long brought back and gone on in France for almost one more 100 years. The government worker turned into an instrument of public power, not the specialist of an individual. This depersonalization of the state supported a fast development in the field of public regulation worried about the association, obligations, and freedoms of "the public power," of which government workers were the chief part. To the arranged construction of the Prussian organization there started to be added the sensible advancement of regulatory regulation.

This bureaucratization was enormously encouraged by Napoleon I, who developed another common help checked not just by a portion of the elements of military association yet in addition by the standards of objectivity, rationale, and comprehensiveness that were the legacy of the Edification. There was a reasonable level of leadership and a solidly settled ordered progression of authorities, with obligations obviously distributed between specialists. Authority was depersonalized and went to the workplace and not the authority — despite the fact that Napoleon demanded that every authority ought to be answerable for move made for the sake of his office. France was partitioned into new regional units: departments, arrondissements, and collectives. In each of these, state government workers had an overall obligation regarding keeping public control, wellbeing, and ethical quality. They were completely connected in a chain to the public Service of the Inside. An extraordinary school, the École Polytechnique, was set up to give the state specialized experts in both the military and the common fields — especially in everyday organization. In the field of general organization, the Conceal d'état ("Chamber of State"), slid from the old Conseil du return on initial capital investment ("Board of the Lord"), forced a scholarly as well as a legal power over the remainder of the common help; as the main significant European regulatory court, it turned into the maker of another sort of managerial law. The eminence of the new French regulatory association and the coherent game plan of its inside structure provoked numerous other European nations to duplicate its chief highlights. What's more, the development of the French Realm spread a large number of its highlights across the world.

In France under the Third Republic (1870-1940) there grew, nonetheless, extensive political obstruction in certain parts of the common help; and quite a bit of its essentialness was decreased as its regulatory practices would in general become clumsy and its staff torpid. Not until 1946 was the framework improved — which included redesigning the managerial design of the focal government, bringing together faculty choice, making a unique service for common help issues, and setting up an extraordinary school, the École Public administration, for the preparation of senior government employees. This school specifically has drawn in overall consideration for its capacity to impart in its alumni both subject matter expert and generalist abilities.

The primary endeavors by Extraordinary England to make productive managerial apparatus emerged from its obligation to oversee India and to keep away from in that country the occasional outrages that undeniable a portion of the standard of the East India Organization. Robert Clive, named legislative head of Bengal for the second time in 1764, presented a code of training that denied workers of the organization from exchanging for their own or tolerating gifts from local brokers. Resulting lead representatives reinforced the boycott, making up for the deficiency of advantages by significantly expanding compensations, presenting advancement by status, and rearranging the higher echelons of organization. Enlistment was carried on by the organization in London, and after 1813 participants to the common help needed to concentrate on the set of experiences, language, and laws of India for a time of four terms at Hailey bury School, Britain, and to get a declaration of acceptable conduct prior to taking up their posts. Because of backing by Thomas Macaulay, secretary to the leading group of control, assessment as opposed to support was embraced as an enrollment strategy. New guidelines from 1833 specified that four applicants must be named for every opening and that they were to contend with each other in "an assessment in such parts of information and by such assessments as the Leading group of the Organization will coordinate."

There was further analysis of how India was run, nonetheless, and in 1853 one more authoritative change of the organization was proposed. The experience of the Indian Common Assistance affected the groundwork of the cutting edge common help in the Assembled Realm. A report was distributed in 1854 on the association of the extremely durable Common Help in England. Its chief creator, Sir Charles Trevelyan, had gained notoriety for looking throughout debasement in the Indian Common Help during 14 years of administration there. The report of 1854 suggested the annulment of support and enrollment by open serious assessment. It further suggested

(1) The foundation of an independent semi judicial group of common assistance magistrates to guarantee the legitimate organization of enrollment to true posts,

(2) the division of crafted by the common help into scholarly and routine work, the two arrangements of workplaces to have separate types of enlistment, and (3) the determination of higher government employees all the more determinedly based on broad scholarly accomplishment than particular information. The Common Help Commission was laid out in 1855, and during the following 30 years support was continuously wiped out. The two unique classes were expanded to four, and a few particular branches were amalgamated to turn into the Logical Common Help. The new respectful help figured out how to draw in to its senior levels profoundly proficient, circumspect, and self-destroying college graduates. Alumni of Oxford and Cambridge became — and stay to the present — particularly unmistakable in the positions of senior government workers in England.

In the US support stayed the standard for significantly longer than in England. From the beginning of the alliance two standards were solidly held. To start with, there was unfriendliness to the thought of a framework of super durable government employees; President Jackson plainly excused this idea of a profoundly proficient station when he said, in 1829, that "the obligations of all open officials are . . . so easy that men of knowledge may promptly qualify themselves for their exhibition." As an outcome, he said, "I cannot however accept that more is lost by the long continuation of men in office than is by and large to be acquired by their experience. Nobody man has any more characteristic right to true station than another." The subsequent rule — that quite far open office ought to be elective — followed pretty much consequently. But since this standard couldn't be basically applied to the subordinate degrees of organization, there fostered the "corruption," in which public office turned into a perquisite of political triumph, being generally used to compensate political help. This framework was defenseless to relentless, glaring, and at last unsatisfactory levels of shortcoming, debasement, and partisanship. These specific shortcomings were unequivocally felt after the nationwide conflict (1861-65), during the time of quick financial and social turn of events. Under extensive strain, the central government acknowledged a limited standard of section by serious open assessment, and in 1883 the U.S. Common Assistance Commission was laid out to control section to office in the government administration. Crafted by the commission was basically confined to the lower grades of work, and it was only after the initial 20 years of the twentieth century that the legitimacy arrangement of enlistment was extended to cover around 50% of the posts in the government administration. After that period the commissions control slowly expanded, predominantly over the lower, center, and administrative workplaces in the government administration. After 1978 the elements of the commission were split between the Workplace of Faculty The executives and the Legitimacy Frameworks Insurance Board. Head strategy causing presents on stay outside the ward of these two bodies, being filled rather by official selection.

The improvement of common help in U.S. nearby government differed among states, regions, and urban areas. The reception of a legitimacy framework can typically be dated from the mid-twentieth 100 years, during the change time of the meddlers. In certain states the legitimacy framework turned out to be deeply grounded, with a focal work force office that incorporated a common help commission or board like the government model. At the other outrageous there was essentially a focal faculty office headed by a solitary work force chief with no warning board. At the civil level, by the mid-twentieth hundred years, most enormous urban communities in the US had fostered a legitimacy arrangement of some kind or another; in more modest urban areas, be that as it may, merit frameworks were correspondingly more uncommon. In the districts, most of which were provincial and had somewhat scarcely any open representatives, officially settled merit frameworks were uncommon.

The Soviet Association

In Russia the Unrest of 1917 cleared away the tsarist common assistance. The Socialist Faction at first held that a solid managerial association will undoubtedly harm the insurgency by hosing immediacy and other progressive excellences. Yet, it before long turned out to be certain that a system devoted to social designing, monetary preparation, and world insurgency required prepared directors. The party fell back, though hesitantly, upon the skill of the more dependable tsarist government workers. It did, in any case, encompass the new thoughtful help with intricate controls trying to guarantee that its individuals stayed faithful to party orders.

As the Socialist Faction it became bureaucratized and as the more excited progressive pioneers were killed, extraordinary modern institutes were set up for party individuals who had shown regulatory ability. With the Initial Five-Year Plan (1928-32) the situation with government employees was improved, and their states of administration were made less inflexible, despite the fact that the party never loosened up its tight arrangement of command over all parts of the state device. In 1935 the State Commission on the Common Assistance was made and connected to the Commissariat of Money with obligation regarding guaranteeing general control of faculty practice. This commission set down conventional examples of managerial construction, changed existing administrative practices, fixed degrees of staffing, normalized frameworks of occupation grouping, and wiped out superfluous capabilities and staff. The inspectorate of the Service of Money guaranteed that the commission's overall approaches were completed in the services. The actual commission stayed under the nearby management of the Committee of Individuals' Commissars to guarantee that it agreed with party orders, and the commission's individuals were designated straight by the chamber.

The Soviet commission, in contrast to those in such nations as Extraordinary England and the US, was given no ward over the enlistment of government employees, which stayed the capability of the services and organizations. The most elevated regulatory and specialized staff individuals were enlisted by every service. Each part of industry and organization had its own preparation schools, from which it chose qualified understudies with palatable records. On arrangement, the understudy was reinforced for at least three years and at risk to criminal procedures assuming that he rejected or in this manner surrendered his task. At the lower levels of organization, enlistment and occupation position were the obligation of the Commissariat of Work Stores.

The Socialist Coalition made decided endeavors to select higher government workers as party individuals. These drives, which trailed behind the

1930s, went far toward changing the actual party into a regulatory and administrative tip top and joining the party and the state organization. The most elevated levels of the common assistance came to comprise a persuasive mechanical assembly and power focus by their own doing. The inner design of the common assistance, also, had been formed along exemplary French and German lines; and titles, positions, emblem, and garbs authoritatively showed up in different pieces of the public administrations.

Individuals' Republic of China additionally showed the contention between progressive doubt of organization and the need to serious areas of strength for develops hardware to achieve progressive objectives. China's long custom of administration stayed significant even after the Socialist Coalition came to control in 1949. In something like 10 years the heaviness of the organization had proactively driven, as per party doctrine, to a hole between the first class and the majority and furthermore to extreme separation among the decision civil servants, or units, themselves. There was not just a differentiation between "old units" and "new frameworks," contingent upon nothing more significant than the date of an authority's entrance into the progressive development, yet in addition a complicated arrangement of occupation assessment that isolated the common help into 24 grades, each with its own position, pay scales, and qualifications. The quantity of appraisals addressed entirely impressive contrasts of force, renown, and privileges and created mental boundaries between the most noteworthy and most reduced grades as perfect and as prominent as between the units and the majority. These differentiations and errors were generally gone after during the Social Unrest of the 1960s and '70s, however they remained profoundly imbued in the managerial design.

Until the seventeenth 100 years, Japan under the shogunate was managed by a military establishmenAfter The Second Great War the United occupation specialists coordinated the entry of a Japanese regulation ensuring that all open authorities ought to be workers of individuals instead of the ruler. The Public Help Law of 1947 set up a free Public Staff Power to manage enrollment, advancement, states of business, principles of execution, and occupation order for the new polite assistance. In fact the ruler himself turned into a government employee, and definite guidelines brought inside the extent of the new regulation all government workers from workers to the state leader. Government workers were characterized into two gatherings, the customary help and an extraordinary help. Government employees in the previous classification entered the help by cutthroat assessment on a standard agreement with residency. The extraordinary help included chosen authorities and political nominees and covered such authorities as individuals from the Eating regimen (council), judges, individuals from the review sheets, and envoys.

Albeit in principle the sovereign individuals had a basic right to pick and excuse every single public authority — that are naturally depicted as "workers of the entire local area" — both custom and political practice permitted the common help in Japan to hold and unite its old situation in government. The romanticizing of the researcher official (a Confucian custom acquired from China) made the common help a free power community. Political battles in the Eating regimen prompted continually evolving services, and individual clergymen seldom remained at a post to the point of laying out firming control of their organization. As in numerous popularity based nations with unpredictable political frameworks, managerial control would in general pass to senior government employees.

Non-industrial countries

Less-created nations have needed to deal with the contrary issue with their common administrations. After The Second Great War numerous such nations became autonomous before they had created viable regulatory designs or assortments of prepared government employees. Not many of the pilgrim powers had prepared native overseers adequately. The English left a feasible managerial design in India and a somewhat Indian zed common help, however the recently free Pakistan had not many experienced government employees. The Belgians left the Congo with practically no prepared managerial or specialized staff, and for certain years there was close to rebellion. comprised of vassals and enfeoffed aristocrats. After the 1630s a common organization created and started to expect a more significant job than the military. Arrangement inside the organization depended on family rank, and authorities were steadfast fundamentally to the primitive ruler. It was only after Matthew C. Perry cruised four U.S. warships into Urara Harbor in 1853, hence effectively finishing over two centuries of Japan's disengagement from the remainder of the world, that the Japanese organization created some distance from primitive position as the premise of arrangements, laying out in its place unwaveringness to the ruler as opposed to medieval masters. Merit arrangements were made on an unassuming scale following Japan was opened toward the West, yet it was only after the 1880s, during the Meiji Rebuilding, that a cutting edge common help was made based on professional stability, vocation ways, and passage by open rivalry. Tokyo College regulation alumni would in general rule this new respectful assistance. Individual devotion to the head was reflected in the situation with Japanese government employees as "Sovereign's Authorities."

In any event, when they acquired sensibly productive regulatory associations, the recently free nations' legislators much of the time demonstrated unequipped for satisfying their allies' assumptions.

Government employees from the old provincial powers who stayed behind frequently found extremist approaches and new bosses unpleasant. The subsequent departure of numerous government employees deteriorated matters, for native government employees were only from time to time a satisfactory substitute.

The absence of qualified work force once in a while prompted a decrease in effectiveness as well as a decrease in regulatory profound quality. Nepotism, tribalism, and defilement as well as shortcoming in the common help were troubles frequently added to different preliminaries of freedom. In numerous nations the inadequacy of the common help was a component prompting military rule, similar to the political downfalls of the chosen chiefs. Military systems were much of the time the final hotel of a nation where the common power neglected to adapt to the issues of freedom. Thusly, the Assembled Countries (UN), related to the states of cutting edge nations, started to foster preparation programs for government employees from immature nations. The principal demand came from Latin America, which prompted the establishing of a school of policy management in Brazil, continued in 1953 by a High level School of Policy implementation for Focal America. Different other global associations, including the Association for Financial Co-activity and Improvement and the World Bank, upheld establishments for the preparation of chairmen in less-created nations. Such establishments incorporated the Middle Easterner Arranging Foundation in Kuwait, the Bedouin Association of Managerial Sciences in Jordan, and the Between American School of Policy implementation in Brazil. Government employees from less-created countries additionally concentrated on organization at such places as the Foundation of Social Examinations in The Hague, the Establishment of Nearby Government Concentrates in Birmingham, Britain, and the Worldwide Organization of Policy implementation in Paris.

After the 1970s the worldwide offices gave less assistance toward preparing, with the understanding — frequently hidden — that the less-created countries would assume on more prominent liability themselves. Preparing additionally would in general be generalist and scholastic, prompting intense deficiencies of prepared managers in particular fields like money and arranging. In any case, associations, for example, the English Gathering started in the mid-1980s to cure a portion of these lacks.

Standards of policy implementation

All through the twentieth century the review and practice of policy implementation was basically sober minded and standardizing instead of hypothetical and worth free. This might make sense of why policy management, in contrast to a few sociologies, created absent a lot of worry about an enveloping hypothesis. Not until the mid-twentieth 100 years and the spread of the German social scientist Max Weber's hypothesis of organization was there much interest in a hypothesis of policy management. Most resulting regulatory hypothesis, nonetheless, was addressed to the confidential area, and there was little work to relate authoritative to political hypothesis.

An unmistakable rule of policy implementation has been economy and productivity — that is, the arrangement of public administrations at the base expense. This has typically been the expressed goal of managerial change. In spite of developing worry about different sorts of values — like responsiveness to public requirements, equity and equivalent treatment, and resident contribution in government choices — productivity keeps on being a significant objective.

In its anxiety with productivity and improvement, policy implementation has zeroed in habitually on inquiries of formal association. It is by and large held that regulatory ills can be to some extent mostly amended by revamping. Numerous hierarchical standards began with the military, a couple from personal business. They incorporate, for instance:

(1) Sorting out divisions, services, and organizations based on normal or firmly related purposes,

(2) Gathering like exercises in single units,

(3) Comparing liability with power,

(4) Guaranteeing solidarity of order (just a single manager for each gathering of workers),

(5) Restricting the quantity of subordinates answering to a solitary boss,

(6) Separating line (working or end-reason) exercises from staff (warning, consultative, or support) exercises,

(7) Utilizing the rule of the executives by exemption (just the uncommon issue or case is brought to the top), and

(8) Having an obvious hierarchy of leadership descending and of obligation vertical.

A few pundits have kept up with that these and different standards of policy implementation are valuable just as unpleasant measures for given hierarchical circumstances. They accept that hierarchical issues vary and that the materialness of rules to different circumstances likewise contrasts. Regardless, and notwithstanding considerably more complex examinations of authoritative conduct in later many years, such standards as those counted above keep on conveying force.

Policy implementation has likewise laid pressure upon faculty. In many nations regulatory change has involved common help change. By and large, the heading has been toward "meritocracy" — the most obviously qualified individual, assessments for section, and choice and advancement based on merit. Consideration has progressively been given to factors other than scholarly legitimacy, including individual perspectives, impetuses, character, individual connections, and aggregate bartering.

What's more, the financial plan has created as a chief device in arranging future projects, choosing needs, overseeing current projects, connecting leader with governing body, and creating control and responsibility. The challenge for command over spending plans, especially in the Western world, started hundreds of years prior and now and again was the fundamental connection among rulers and their subjects. The advanced chief spending plan framework in which the leader suggests, the council appropriates, and the leader manages consumptions began in nineteenth century England. In the US during the twentieth hundred years, the financial plan turned into the central vehicle for authoritative observation of organization, chief control of divisions, and departmental control of subordinate projects. It plays expected a comparative part in a considerable lot of the non-industrial nations of the world.

The traditional way to deal with policy implementation depicted above most likely arrived at its fullest improvement in the US during the 1930s, despite the fact that since that time, through instructive and preparing programs, specialized help, and crafted by worldwide associations, it has likewise become standard regulation in numerous nations. Be that as it may, a portion of its components have been opposed by legislatures with English or mainland legitimate viewpoints, and in any event, during the 1930s it was being tested from a few quarters. Since that time investigation of the subject has extraordinarily evolved.

The conventional principle laid on the reason that organization was just the execution of not set in stone by others. As per this view, heads ought to look for greatest proficiency yet ought to be generally nonpartisan about values and objectives. During the Economic crisis of the early 20s of the 1930s, and, surprisingly, more so during The Second Great War, nonetheless, it turned out to be progressively apparent that numerous new approaches started inside the organization, that arrangement and worth decisions were implied in most huge managerial choices, that numerous regulatory authorities dealt with nothing with the exception of strategy, and that, to the extent that public strategies were questionable, such work unavoidably elaborate directors in legislative issues. The alleged freedom of organization from strategy and legislative issues supposedly was deceptive. Since the 1930s there has accordingly been expanding worry with strategy arrangement and the advancement of procedures to further develop strategy choices. Albeit the idea of a worth free, impartial organization is viewed by quite a few people as at this point not valid, no completely good substitute has been advertised. The most effective method to guarantee that mindful and responsive strategy choices are made via profession executives, and how to facilitate their work with the approaches of politically chosen or representative authorities, stay key distractions, particularly in fair states.

It was with legislative endeavors to battle the Downturn that new enlightening gadgets were presented, including public pay bookkeeping and the examination of gross public item as a significant file of monetary wellbeing. The applied strategies of financial and money related strategy have become laid out specializations of policy management. Business analysts possess key posts in the organizations of most countries, and numerous different managers should have essentially rudimentary information on the financial ramifications of government activities. France, Sweden and other Scandinavian countries, Extraordinary England, and the US were among the forerunners in creating monetary arranging strategies. Such arranging has turned into a ruling worry of policy management in a significant number of the non-industrial nations.

As financial and social intercession by legislatures has expanded, the impediments of "incrementalism" as a policy implementation practice have become progressively clear. Incrementalism is the inclination of government to dabble with strategies instead of to scrutinize the benefit of proceeding with them. Various strategies have been acquainted with settle on choices more reasonable. One such strategy, broadly applied, is money saving advantage examination. This includes distinguishing, evaluating, and looking at the expenses and advantages of elective recommendations. Another, less effective, method was the Preparation, Programming, and Planning Framework (PPBS), brought into the U.S. Branch of Protection in 1961 and stretched out to the government spending plan in 1965. As per PPBS, the goals of taxpayer supported initiatives were to be recognized, and afterward elective method for accomplishing these targets were to be contrasted concurring with their expenses and advantages. Practically speaking, PPBS had little effect in administrative planning, part of the way in light of the fact that the targets of legislative projects were hard to determine and mostly in light of the fact that thorough assessment took excessively lengthy. PPBS were deserted in 1971, and comparative endeavors, like Administration by Targets and Zero-Base Planning, both presented during the 1970s, were similarly brief and insufficient. Similar plans in Western Europe, for example, the technique called "legitimization of monetary decision" brought into France in the last part of the 1960s and the supposed Program Examination and Audit in Extraordinary England during the 1970s, were moreover fruitless.

Quantitative financial estimation is helpful in a limited way, yet the worth of human existence, of independence from disorder and torment, of security in the city, of clean air, and of chance for accomplishment are not really quantifiable in money related terms. Policy management has accordingly progressively worried about growing better friendly pointers, quantitative and subjective — that is, better lists of the impacts of public projects and new methods of social examination.

Advancement has been a rising accentuation on human relations. This began during the 1930s when what became known as the Hawthorne research, including the specialists and the board of a modern plant close to Chicago, drew out the significance to efficiency of social or casual association, great interchanges, individual and gathering conduct, and perspectives (as particular from aptitudes).

Attention to the significance of human relations impacted the lead of policy management. Numerous customs of organization (progressive system, mandate authority, set obligations, treatment of representatives as generic "units" of creation, and money related impetuses) were tested.

By the last part of the 1930s the human relations approach had formed into an idea known as "association improvement." Its essential objective was to change the perspectives, values, and designs of associations with the goal that they could fulfill new needs. Prepared advisors, as a rule from outside the association, embraced serious talking of senior and junior staff, and responsiveness preparing and conflict gatherings were likewise held. Dissimilar to the rationalistic PPBS approach, association advancement focused on the distinguishing proof of individual with hierarchical objectives, the "self-completion" of laborers and administrators, viable relational correspondence, and expansive support in navigation. Its immediate use inside legislative organizations has been restricted and has not forever been effective; however it has had extensive circuitous impact upon executives.

One more present day development in policy implementation has been the more prominent support of residents in government. It was invigorated during the 1950s and '60s by a developing inclination that states were not answering the requirements of their residents, especially minority gatherings and poor people. Different examinations to include residents or their delegates in pursuing administrative choices were started during the 1960s. These elaborate the assignment of decision making from integral to neighborhood workplaces and, at the nearby level, the imparting of power to resident gatherings.

Public strategy approach

From the mid-1970s expanding examination of the manner in which government strategies impacted the public brought about an idea called the "public strategy approach" to organization. This looks at how much each stage in conceiving and executing a strategy influences the general shape and effect of the strategy. As per the idea, how an issue is imagined in any case impacts the scope of cures considered. The idea of the dynamic cycle might decide if a game-plan is only gradual or really extremist. Without a doubt, it has been contended that the idea of the dynamic cycle shapes the result of the actual choice, especially when the interaction is overwhelmed by a strong vested party. In addition, the eagerness of the public authority to assess programs, and adjust them if essential, influences the result. Numerous allies of the public strategy approach view the idea as a significant instrument for building a group of information on which proposals can be based.

Until The Second Great War there was somewhat little trade among countries of thoughts regarding policy implementation. As soon as 1910, notwithstanding, an expert association, which in the long run turned into the Worldwide Foundation of Regulatory Sciences (IIAS), had been laid out. At first its participation comprised basically of researchers and professionals of regulatory regulation in the nations of mainland Europe. By the last part of the 1980s the IIAS had an enrollment drawn from exactly 70 nations. Its third congresses take care of all parts of the field.

Since The Second Great War global interest in regulatory frameworks has developed, encouraged by the need of participation during the conflict, by the arrangement of worldwide associations, by the control of vanquished countries and the organization of financial recuperation programs for Europe and the East Asia, and by help programs for emerging nations. One side-effect of help programs was a reestablished enthusiasm for how urgent compelling organization is to public turn of events. It has additionally become evident how parochial and culture-bound styles of policy management have frequently stayed inside individual nations.

One more impact of this worldwide correspondence and sharing of encounters has been the acknowledgment that advancement isn't select to the alleged immature nations. All nations have proceeded to create, and policy management has progressively been seen as the organization of arranged change in social orders that themselves have gone through quick change, not every last bit of it arranged. Government has never again been simply the guardian of the harmony and the supplier of essential administrations: in the postindustrial period government has turned into a main trailblazer, a determinant of social and monetary needs, and a business visionary on a significant scale. On essentially every critical issue or challenge — from joblessness to clean air — individuals have sought the public authority for arrangements or help. The undertakings of arranging, putting together, planning, making due and assessing current government have moreover become wonderful in both aspect and significance.

European colleges have customarily delivered authoritative attorneys for their state run administrations, however legitimate abilities alone are not really satisfactory for dealing with contemporary issues. U.S. colleges started graduate projects in the early long stretches of the twentieth 100 years, and by the last part of the 1980s there were in excess of 300 college programs in policy implementation. By and by, not many of the researchers and different experts who become executives in their fields go to such projects.

Preparing programs have especially thrived since The Second Great War, large numbers of them with government help. Some are connected to colleges. In laying out the École National administration as one of its polite help changes of 1946-47, France gave a broad course to volunteers to the higher common help. It was only after 1969 that England laid out a Common Help School under the new Considerate Assistance Division. In the US the public authority laid out an assortment of instructive and preparing programs during the 1960s, including the Government Leader Establishment and the Chief Workshop Communities. Some less-high level nations have since laid out places for the preparation of public managers.

Baby and baby wellbeing, area of medication worried about the prosperity and avoidance of sickness among youngsters ages 0 to three years.

Perhaps of the main figure advancing baby wellbeing is bosom taking care of, which gives solid wellbeing assurance to newborn children and enjoys the benefit of being more advantageous and less expensive than bottle-taking care of. In less-created nations, small kids are much of the time bosom took care of for broadened periods since bosom milk is their essential wellspring of sustenance. Both the World Wellbeing Association (WHO) and the Assembled Countries Kids' Asset (UNICEF) support bosom taking care of for something like two years. In created nations, most babies are weaned toward the finish of their most memorable year of life, while possibly not sooner. The level of ladies who decide to bosom feed additionally fluctuates by country. For instance, bosom taking care of rates are all around as high as 98% in Sweden; in nations with such high rates, government strategies frequently are intended to energize the training. In the US most of ladies bosom feed babies, and about half proceed with bosom taking care of until the child is a half year old. Working moms who decide to can utilize a bosom siphon to communicate bosom milk to be taken care of to babies by different guardians. Strong food sources are presented as educated by pediatricians, starting with cereals and advancing to vegetables, natural products, and meats. By 8 to a year, babies might eat delicate or pureed table food.

Graphing development and forestalling sickness

Babies and little children visit clinical consideration suppliers at assigned stretches to have their development and advancement diagrammed, to get inoculations, to have hearing and vision checked, and to have potential issues recognized. UNICEF gauges that 1.4 million kids under age five pass on every year from immunization preventable infections. Inoculations that safeguard youngsters from different preventable irresistible infections are accessible at doctors' workplaces and at wellbeing centers around the world. Required inoculations by and large incorporate diphtheria, pertussis (outshining hack), lockjaw, polio, measles, mumps, rubella (German measles), Hemophilic flu type B (Hob), hepatitis B, and chicken pox. A few schools might decline to enlist a kid who has not gotten the necessary vaccinations. In less-created nations, worldwide associations, for example, UNICEF and WHO frequently work with neighborhood states to advance vaccination programs.

Inoculations, be that as it may, don't go about as obstructions to visit ear, respiratory, and gastrointestinal diseases. Typically, these contaminations answer well to treatment and are not foundations for critical concern. Notwithstanding, microbes that are answerable for specific ear diseases (otitis media) seem, by all accounts, to be creating protection from normal anti-microbial.

Constant ear diseases have been related with extremely durable hearing harm. In like manner, while weak babies and little children have looseness of the bowels, they are defenseless to lack of hydration, which, whenever left untreated, could prompt passing. Rehydration recipes are generally accessible to reestablish liquids and electrolytes.

Kids in financially impeded families will quite often be in less fortunate wellbeing than those in everybody. In certain spots, paces of lead and pesticide poisonings might be higher in this fragment of the populace, however all youngsters are powerless to harming in hazardous conditions. Newborn children and babies in less-created nations, where sterilization and admittance to safe water and food might be restricted, are profoundly helpless to a large group of waterborne and food-borne sicknesses, like typhoid fever and cholera, and to vector-borne illnesses, like intestinal sickness and dengue fever.

Either upon entering the world or presently, a baby might give the primary indication of a sent illness or an acquired irregularity. For example, babies brought into the world to HIV-positive moms might become contaminated with HIV upon entering the world. Certain acquired metabolic problems, like phenylketonuria, are analyzed at or not long after birth, as is fetal liquor disorder, a condition brought about by extreme maternal admission of liquor during pregnancy. Numerous hereditary and inherent problems can be analyzed prenatally through screening. In any case, early showing advances may not be accessible to or effortlessly got to by pregnant ladies in a few less-created nations.

Admittance to clinical consideration and appropriate sustenance are vital for the typical development and advancement of babies (0 to a year) and little children (12 to three years). Newborn child mortality is one of the main signs of the degree of social advancement inside every country. Subsequently, death rates will more often than not be lower in created nations and higher in less-created nations. The most noteworthy baby death rates are tracked down in Angola, Afghanistan, and numerous nations in sub-Saharan Africa. On the other hand, Monaco, Japan, Bermuda, and Singapore are among the nations with the most minimal newborn child death rates. Starting around 1990 most nations have encountered decreases in baby death rates. Perinatal (inside the primary month of life) death rates have additionally declined, because of upgrades in clinical information and innovation and expanded consideration paid to pre-birth care and baby wellbeing. Likewise, the frequencies of low-birth-weight babies and short-gestational births have dropped in certain nations, in this way assisting with working on the by and large measurable soundness of enduring newborn children and little children.

Unexpected newborn child passing disorder (SIDS) is a typical reason for death among baby's ages two weeks to one year — surprising passing's of ostensibly solid newborn children. SIDS is analyzed in situations where not an obvious reason of death arises following examination and dissection. It seems to happen with expanded rate in babies presented to tobacco smoke and among newborn children with low birth weight. The mission to put dozing babies on their backs has assisted with lessening the pace of SIDS.

Further developing newborn child and baby wellbeing

Missions to further develop baby and little child wellbeing frequently have explicit objectives, for example, decreasing iron inadequacy and poisonings, diminishing development hindrance related with different causes, or lessening the pace of anti-infection use for ear diseases. Cutting the pace of newborn child mortality, remembering decreases for SIDS rates, and further developing availability to immunizations and rehydration treatments are objectives normal to nations around the world. The utilization of vehicle seats and the end of lead from paints utilized in youngsters' toys are different areas of worry for newborn child and baby wellbeing and security.

Wet-nursing, the act of bosom taking care of another's baby. In specific times of history and among a few social levels, wet-nursing was a paid calling. The historical backdrop of wet-nursing is antiquated (dating to maybe 3000 BCE) and inescapable. It went on as training into the 21st 100 years, however in many regions of the planet information on its potential risks has made it even more an act of need as opposed to of comfort or eminence.

Explanations behind utilizing a wet medical caretaker have not changed throughout the long term. Until the improvement of baby bottles and their sanitization and the development of newborn child recipe, it was the most secure, easiest, and most ideal choice for keeping newborn children, who require the supplements found in bosom milk, alive. If, as her very own result disease, passing, or insufficient or bombed lactation, a mother couldn't take care of her baby, a wet medical attendant would be utilized. Frequently more well-off families involved wet medical caretakers as an issue of the mother's comfort. As labor, parenthood, and youngster rising became musicalized, the once-normal act of wet-nursing started to decline. In most evolved nations — on the grounds that medications, liquor, and infections, for example, HIV and other possibly harming matter can be passed to a baby through bosom milk — the act of wet-nursing has been generally supplanted by the utilization of newborn child recipe. In locales where different options are scant, wet-nursing keeps on being normal.

The act of cross-nursing, where a lady bosom takes care of both her kid and another, is at times utilized, most regularly for motivations behind youngster care or looking after children.

Weariness, explicit type of human deficiency in which the singular encounters an abhorrence for effort and feels unfit to continue. Such sentiments might be created by solid exertion; weariness of the energy supply to the muscles of the body, in any case, is definitely not a constant forerunner. Sensations of weariness may likewise come from torment, uneasiness, dread, or fatigue. In the last option cases, muscle capability generally is healthy.

The once-held conviction that work was the reason for weariness prompted endeavors to utilize the work result of assembly line laborers, for instance, as immediate proportions of exhaustion. Early examinations by modern clinicians and designers neglected to show a nearby association between how a singular specialist said he felt and how much work he achieved; creation situated agents were even prompted property no importance by any means to inward sensations of weakness, and their consideration moved from the internal state of the laborer to outside peculiarities not connected with the laborer by any stretch of the imagination. In the process it was failed to remember that work yield is a result of, as opposed to a portrayal of, the specialist.

The historical backdrop of general wellbeing is gotten from numerous authentic thoughts, experimentation, the advancement of fundamental sciences, innovation, and the study of disease transmission. In the advanced time, James Lind's clinical preliminary of different dietary medicines of English mariners with scurvy in 1756 and Edward Jenner's 1796 revelation that cowpox immunization forestalls smallpox have cutting edge applications as the science and practices of nourishment and vaccination are urgent impacts on wellbeing among the populaces of creating and created nations.

History gives a point of view to foster a comprehension of medical issues of networks and how to adapt to them. We imagine through the eyes of the past how social orders conceptualized and managed infection. All social orders should confront the real factors of illness and passing, and foster ideas and techniques to oversee them. These methodologies advanced from logical information and experimentation, however are related with social and cultural circumstances, convictions and practices that are significant in deciding wellbeing status and therapeutic and preventive mediations to further develop wellbeing.

The historical backdrop of general wellbeing is an account of the quest for successful method for getting wellbeing and forestalling sickness in the populace. Pandemic and endemic irresistible illness invigorated thought and development in sickness counteraction on an even minded premise, frequently before the causation was laid out experimentally. The anticipation of illness in populaces spins around characterizing sicknesses, estimating their event, and looking for successful mediations.

General wellbeing advanced through experimentation and with extending logical clinical information, now and again dubious, frequently invigorated by war and cataclysmic events. The requirement for coordinated wellbeing security developed as a feature of the improvement of local area life, and specifically, urbanization and social changes. Strict and cultural convictions impacted ways to deal with making sense of and endeavoring to control transferable infection by disinfection, town arranging, and arrangement of clinical consideration. Religions and social frameworks have likewise seen logical examination and the spread of information as undermining, bringing about restraint of advancements in general wellbeing, with present day instances of resistance to contraception, vaccination, and food fortress.

Logical debates, like the contagionist and anticontagionist controversies during the nineteenth hundred years and resistance to social change developments, were brutal and brought about lengthy postpones in reception of the accessible logical information. Such discussions went on into the 20th nevertheless go on into the twenty-first hundred years with a merging of philosophies shown to be intelligent consolidating the sociologies, wellbeing advancement, and translational sciences bringing the most ideal that anyone could hope to find proof of science and practice together for more prominent viability in strategy improvement for individual and populace wellbeing rehearses.

Current culture in high, medium low pay nations actually faces the antiquated scourges of transferable sicknesses, yet additionally the advanced pandemics of cardiovascular infection, malignant growths, psychological maladjustment, and injury. The development of AIDS (Helps), extreme intense respiratory disorder (SARS), avian flu, and medication safe microorganisms compels us to look for better approaches for forestalling their possibly serious outcomes to society. Dangers to wellbeing in a world confronting serious environment and biological change present brutal and possibly destroying ramifications for society.

The development of general wellbeing is a proceeding with process; microbes change, as do the climate and the host. To confront the difficulties ahead, having a comprehension of the past is significant. In spite of the fact that there is a lot of in this age that is new, large numbers of the ongoing discussions and contentions in general wellbeing are reverberations of the past. Experience from the past is an essential device in the plan of wellbeing strategy. A comprehension of the advancement and setting of those difficulties and creative thoughts can assist us with exploring the general wellbeing universe of today and what's in store.

The historical backdrop of general wellbeing strategy focuses to instances of proof based approach as well as various occasions where arrangements don't appear to be proof based. It very well may be contended, for example, that the evil impacts of tobacco on smoking were known during the 1950s, yet strategy activity was generally negligible until the 1980s and ahead. Additionally, in spite of the fact that there are instances of effective practices in HIV counteraction and control (like in Australia), numerous nations still can't seem to take on proof based strategies.

Speculations about the approach making process, which integrate acknowledgment of the governmental issues of independent direction, begin to give a few responses to why proof isn't occupied 100% of the time. There are, nonetheless, different impacts that shape general wellbeing strategy making. Given general wellbeing strategy settling on worries making a conclusion about what is useful for the general public overall, there are endless variables to be thought of: the sufficiency and culmination of proof; the potential advantages and results (and their dissemination); how to compromise present moment and long haul expenses and gains; and how to accommodate possibly clashing social qualities, social convictions, and customs, institutional and political designs, and cycles for strategy making. Consequently, decision making at the populace level is more unsure (Do brow et al., 2004) and it are at any point present to contend requests of partners. Chiefs might be gone up against with both moral and instructive vulnerability, as the meaning of the issue, the potential arrangements, and the idea of proof that supports both are challenged. Strategy making, by its tendency, requires pursuing decisions that are not esteem free or reducible to specialized inputs (Rodin, 2001).

Also, strategy creators might have objectives other than clinical adequacy while delivering wellbeing strategy. Wellbeing administration arrangements, which ought to at last work on clinical results, might be made with monetary, social, or key advancement objectives as a top priority (Dark, 2001). Networks take on various originations of wellbeing risk (Beck,

1992), and these ideas of hazard might be formed by broad communications portrayal of occasions. Media can likewise make political gamble by focusing on discusses or famous worries (Davies and Marshall, 2000; Marshall et al., 2005). Likewise, the discussion about strategy decisions might be covered as clashing points of view about proof (Atkins et al., 2005). Legislative issues, philosophy, and political economy may in this manner be more significant drivers of strategy making, particularly when there is logical and strategy vulnerability about the fitting course of strategy activity.

Past political intricacies, there are likewise functional boundaries to confirm based wellbeing strategy making. Indeed, even with the best expectations, it has not forever been workable for scientists and strategy creators to associate the consequences of examination with direction. Scientists and strategy creators have been portrayed as living in two universes (Lomas, 2000). There are various contrasts between these two gatherings as far as objectives and styles in navigation (Buse et al., 2005; Choi et al., 2005; Brownson et al., 2006) (Table 4).

Strategy producers are known to grumble that they can't acquire research proof when they need or need it, and that what is accessible frequently doesn't address the approach question of concern. These deterrents have recently been featured as the basic holes needing arrangement (Dark, 2001). In any event, when the discoveries are convenient, for strategy purposes, strategy producers may not realize how best to utilize the data. Weiss (1991) recommends that exploration results might be delegated:

(1) Information and discoveries,

(2) Thoughts and analysis, and

(3) Contentions for activity, each being seen to be helpful for various purposes. Research information and discoveries might be valuable for picking strategy choices when the idea of the arrangement issues and potential arrangements are clear. Thoughts and reactions might be more valuable for strategy plan setting, to acquire consideration on approach issues and potential arrangements. Contentions for activity, notwithstanding, are probably going to require

dynamic support by those engaged with the strategy making process.

The historical backdrop of general wellbeing frequently causes to notice its starting points related to utilitarianism, with an accentuation on further developing wellbeing results as a component of everyone's benefit. Steven Holland has significantly brought up, nonetheless, that utilitarian examinations in general wellbeing would do well to keep away from gullible utilitarianism that just weighs results with regards to their effects on wellbeing (i.e., their probability to increment or decline horribleness and mortality). The guideline of utility expresses that activities are correct to the extent that they advance the best bliss for society. A more refined utilitarian investigation ought to consider short-and long haul results; various types of results past those of wellbeing; and whether specific activities or basic guidelines advance the most bliss, as taking on an alternate degree of examination can some of the time propose clashing strategy suggestions (Holland, 2007). For instance, it could help the larger part to isolation a couple of residents, regardless of whether there is a slim likelihood of contamination. But since residents could see such activity as forfeiting the couple of for the numerous as unreasonable, it might deliver improved ramifications for society on the off chance that strategy producers keep a more basic principle not to fall back on general wellbeing compulsion when the probability of mischief is more sure.

As well as planning to boost general wellbeing, the most predominant component of utilitarianism in general wellbeing morals is work of the mischief rule exactly for the reasons for legitimizing coercive general wellbeing measures, for example, separation of the debilitated, quarantine of the uncovered, or compulsory immunization. The mischief standard expresses that "the main reason for which power can be legitimately practiced over any individual from a socialized local area, despite his desire to the contrary, is to forestall damage to other people" (Factory, 1998). The primary test for general wellbeing practice is to figure out what sorts of damages and how possible they should be to legitimize a conjuring of the mischief guideline. Are financial weights that outcome from undesirable ways of behaving enough? Is a microbe with low transmission rates yet high mortality sufficiently hazardous to legitimize compulsion? And the opposite? Such inquiries demonstrate that how one deciphers that hurt standard can bring about various proposals for general wellbeing strategy.

Likewise, the impediments of a utilitarian examination, as well as the outcome of different methodologies in applied morals, propose that no general wellbeing morals will be (or should be) limited to one moral custom, as each tends to reveal insight into critical highlights of the ethical scene (Callahan and Jennings, 2002; Roberts and Reich, 2002). A focus on general wellbeing morals over the most recent twenty years has brought about a plenty of new structures explicitly intended for wrestling with general wellbeing challenges. For instance, Nancy Kass has fostered an outstanding six-step structure for general wellbeing morals, including distinguishing program objectives, assessing viability, recognizing loads forced by the program, distinguishing methodologies for limiting said troubles, and guaranteeing that the program is carried out decently (Kass, 2001). Somewhere else, a few creators utilize different moral customs to limn the conceivable outcomes of the field, while yet others cause to notice the social idea of general wellbeing as populace wellbeing can uncover high levels of human interdependency (Childress et al., 2002; Bailys et al., 2008). Such outlines mirror the variety of moral assets that can be brought to bear inside morals of general wellbeing, yet in addition the intricacy of the actual calling; its assorted and dissimilar exercises might require moral examinations of various types, and on various levels.

General Wellbeing Approaches Not Necessarily in all cases Proof Informed)?

The historical backdrop of general wellbeing strategy focuses to instances of proof informed arrangement as well as various cases where approaches miss the mark on proof base. It very well may be contended, for example, that the evil impacts of tobacco on smoking were known during the 1950s, yet strategy activity was generally negligible until the 1980s and ahead. Essentially, albeit the medical problems related with heftiness and unfortunate nourishment are all around perceived, proof informed arrangement reactions are moderately interesting and efficient

Speculations about the strategy making process, which consolidate acknowledgment of the governmental issues of direction, begin to give a few responses with regards to why proof isn't occupied all of the time. There are various impacts that shape general wellbeing strategy making. Considering that the focal point of general wellbeing strategy is to drive choices helpful for society overall, there are many elements to be thought of: the ampleness and fulfillment of proof; the potential advantages and outcomes (and their circulation); how to compromise present moment and long haul expenses and gains; and how to accommodate possibly clashing financial interests, social qualities, social convictions, and customs, institutional and political designs, and cycles for strategy making.

In this way, decision-production at the populace level is in many cases taken in a milieu of vulnerability (Do brow et al., 2004) and it are at any point present to contend requests of partners. Networks take on various originations of wellbeing risk (Beck, 1992), and these thoughts of hazard might be formed by broad communications portrayal of occasions. Media can likewise make political gamble by pointing out discusses or well-known concerns (Davies and Marshall, 2000; Marshall et al., 2005). Likewise, the discussion about approach decisions might be covered as clashing viewpoints about proof (Atkins et al., 2005). Chiefs might be gone up against with both moral and educational vulnerability, as the meaning of the issue, the potential arrangements, and the idea of proof that supports both are challenged.

Furthermore, strategy creators might have objectives other than viability with respect to wellbeing results while delivering wellbeing strategy. Wellbeing administration approaches, which ought to eventually work on clinical results, might be made with monetary, social, or key improvement objectives as a top priority (Dark, 2001). Via model, general wellbeing arrangements, especially those focusing on risk factors for constant infection, as often as possible intercede available through tax collection or guideline. Extract charges forced on sugar-improved drinks or a scope of food varieties and refreshments considered unfortunate might fill the twofold need of decreasing utilization and raising general or wellbeing explicit income. The brief Danish expense on immersed fat substance delineates the problem of such a twofold reason where the objectives are not really 100 percent harmonious: the plan of the Danish duty was viewed as lumbering and outlandish, to a limited extent in light of the fact that specific standards didn't appear to focus on wellbeing results, yet rather underscored expanding income assortment (Vallgårda et al., 2015). Experts contend that the way that the duty was important for a bigger monetary change bundle that continued through monetary instead of wellbeing dynamic designs added to its fast nullification since it permitted the political and public talk to move quickly from addressing wellbeing worries to a conversation of unfriendly financial effect and forestalled general wellbeing advocates from strongly supporting the expense (Bødker et al., 2015; Vallgårda et al., 2015). Legislative issues, philosophy, and political economy may hence be more significant drivers of strategy making, particularly when there is logical and strategy vulnerability about the suitable course of strategy activity.

Past political intricacies, there are additionally functional obstructions to prove informed wellbeing strategy making. Indeed, even with the best aims, it has not forever been workable for scientists and strategy producers to interface the consequences of exploration with navigation. Analysts and strategy creators have been portrayed as living in two universes (Lomas, 2000). There are various contrasts between these two gatherings regarding goals and styles in choice.

Indeed, even where efficient surveys of proof do exist, general wellbeing leaders might in any case experience various difficulties in integrating them into direction. These incorporate finding important proof and basic examinations of that proof, the idealness of proof gave and the trouble in realizing how best to utilize the data (Tireless, 2011). Weiss (1991) proposes that examination results might be delegated (1) information and discoveries,

(2) Thoughts and analysis, and

(3) Contentions for activity, each being seen to be valuable for various purposes. Research information and discoveries might be valuable for picking strategy choices when the idea of the approach issues and potential arrangements are clear. Thoughts and reactions might be more helpful for strategy plan setting, to acquire consideration on arrangement

issues and give potential arrangements. Contentions for activity, nonetheless, are probably going to require dynamic support by those associated with the approach making process.

Notwithstanding the accessibility and reasonableness of exploration proof for strategy making, it ought to be noticed that even a decent proof base doesn't naturally convert into effective strategy execution. As Rotten (2012) calls attention to "in the event that these strategies come up short [...] to move toward key determinants of successful strategy advancement and execution," because of reasons, for example, lacking hierarchical limit or inability to consider political contemplations and popular assessment, their substance might be proof based, yet they won't arrive at anticipated objectives.

Early General Wellbeing and Early Cleanliness

Chips away at the historical backdrop of general wellbeing are in many cases rather short with regards to the improvement of the field in antiquated times. In the old style 535-page A Past filled with General

Wellbeing (1993), George Rosen has proactively entered the Medieval times by page 26; and moreover the point 'Wellbeing and profound quality in the old world' has been given a simple 12-page section by Dorothy Doorman in her Wellbeing, Development and the State (1999), which covers 376 pages.

Nonetheless, there might be valid justifications for that. Contingent upon how the idea of general wellbeing is deciphered, one might contend that the idea of general wellbeing, as the articulation is utilized today, started in the eighteenth 100 years, a point likewise examined by Doorman (1993). Maybe interest in the ailments of populaces with an expectation of dynamic mediation to improve the aggregate wellbeing is basically posterity of the Illumination. This social foundation might be seen as an overall essential for general wellbeing, regardless of whether a few estimates that are viewed as a feature of the present general wellbeing field are seen as additional back ever, like frameworks for offering clinical benefits and quarantine in the event of plagues. Assuming we view cleanliness as the logical field that targets dealing with wellbeing among the sound, general wellbeing is cleanliness applied on the total level to safeguard wellbeing for the gathering and not basically for the individual (Brockington, 1960). In course books of cleanliness one frequently finds outings into the historical backdrop of the field where the two ideas are dealt with together. For instance, Hueppe (1925) saw the improvement of general wellbeing pretty much as a continuum that began in days of yore.

After the Greek wellbeing goddess, Hygeia, little girl of Asklepios and sister of the goddess for the treatment of illnesses, Panakeia (Leven, 2005), turned out to be essential for the Asklepios love culture from the fifth century BC, the field of cleanliness was named after her. 'Cleanliness' implied then, yet does, rules and guidance for the conservation of wellbeing both on the singular level and on the public level; that is, mediation when illnesses undermine, covering public fields, for example, waste of sumps which were viewed as undesirable, control of wells and different types of water supply, city arranging, food dealing with, diet, and neatness, as well as measures against individual infections viewed as dangers to the populace.

The logical foundation of cleanliness lies on the overarching speculations for causation of infection and on the impression of wellbeing perils, yet in addition on the perspectives on the linkages among wellbeing and society (Sigerist, 1945). In days of yore, wellbeing was firmly connected to the comprehension of the world thusly and subsequently must be deciphered inside this structure (Sigerist, 1960a,b). Observational information was just essential for the reason for cleanliness, as different impression of wellbeing and sickness frequently involved a focal spot in the personalities of individuals; for instance, illness because of enchanted impacts, illness because of activities by an underhanded soul, infection as vengeance, or infection as discipline for infringement of municipal guidelines or for culpable strict principles. Likewise, these wellbeing gambles required the preventive estimates that had a place with the field of cleanliness of the time (Hinnels and Watchman, 1999). Sterile measures, on both the individual and aggregate levels, not just saved wellbeing and prosperity as per contemporary originations, yet in addition had different capabilities, for example, ensuring individuals acted as per the guidelines of society and in accordance with requests set by religion. Many guidelines, measures, and propensities associated with religion might be clean in character, however in any case have a place with a circle other than general wellbeing. In this way, cleanliness ever, particularly the general wellbeing side of it, should frequently to some extent be seen as a determinant for the conservation of the specific culture to which it had a place.

Medicinal natural techniques guarantees more noteworthy wellbeing insurance

The historical backdrop of general wellbeing progress has demonstrated that the broadest and best general medical advantages are gotten from medicinal or preventive estimates taken by a focal power and including natural intercessions that bring down the degree of openness of enormous populaces to ecologically sent sickness. Such measures as focal plants for the decontamination of drinking water supplies, sanitization of milk, and region wide lobbies for decreasing the reproducing destinations of intestinal sickness conveying mosquitoes are notable instances of accomplishment utilizing this technique. Any healing activity in light of changing individual way of behaving and way of life through training, policing, both, is a lot more slow cycle and, as a general rule, has succeeded exclusively in regions with moderately high instructive levels and expectations for everyday comforts.

The wastewater stockpiling and treatment/stockpiling supply choice audited above offers this sort of midway overseen and designed type of healing ecological intercession. The main medicinal measure will all the while decrease the negative wellbeing impacts for sewage ranch laborers and for the public that drinks wastewater-inundated vegetables. Likewise the no one but measure can achieve medical advantages in a brief time frame without huge changes in private way of behaving or prohibitive guidelines that rely upon complex examination and policing. Notwithstanding, it requires focal authoritative and the board limit, accessibility of major monetary assets and accessibility of land.

In spite of the fact that it could be proper in certain circumstances to limit the sort of harvests developed or to control wastewater water system rehearses, such guidelines are challenging to implement where there is overwhelming interest in salad yields and nursery vegetables. In dry and semi-dry zones (as well as a few muggy regions), where water system is exceptionally alluring, numerous financial experts and farming specialists consider it monetarily judicious to permit unlimited wastewater water system of money crops popular. That objective must be accomplished with a successful elevated degree of wastewater treatment as proposed in this section.

The Starting points of the General Wellbeing Calling

The historical backdrop of general wellbeing lets us know that the significant enhancements in the soundness of populaces have come about not through the endeavors of clinical frameworks orientated toward the consideration of people with explicit illnesses yet through the improvement of general social circumstances, for example, lodging, food supply and quality, water, and disinfection (see Figure 1). Albeit this is a verifiable viewpoint, being chiefly connected with the nineteenth century sterile upheaval that began in Britain during the 1830s and

1840s, the ascent in the significance of noncommunicable sicknesses worldwide, including weight, diabetes, and liquor/tobacco-related illnesses, has underlined the significance of essential counteraction. What might be compared to the clean development is revolved around the social determinants of wellbeing.

In the UK, the historical backdrop of expert commitment with general wellbeing in an organized manner traces all the way back to the mid-nineteenth century when the post of Clinical Official of Wellbeing (MOH) was made among the English nearby specialists. The principal MOHs were for the most part parttime, who joined the neighborhood authority post with clinical practice. The primary proper capability in general wellbeing was the Recognition in State Medication that was organized in 1871 by Trinity School in Dublin. The breath of general wellbeing concern was represented by the consideration in the schedule of subjects like measurements, meteorology, and designing. It was only after the mid-20th century that the ownership of an expert capability in general wellbeing became necessary in England for those holding the MOH post.

Other related capabilities, for example, those granted to sterile assessors, grew independently however at the same time with the clinical world.

In the USA, the main general wellbeing structures came in to being in the last part of the nineteenth 100 years in the port urban communities on the East coast. By the 1870s and 1880s, most States had laid out their own general wellbeing structures. It was industrialization and fast populace development that prodded the improvement of general wellbeing in the huge urban communities, similarly as it had occurred in Britain.

It was the beginning of the Public Wellbeing Administration (NHS) across the UK in 1948 that made various strands of clinical commitment with populace medical problems. The vitally proficient general wellbeing staffing, and an extensive variety of general wellbeing administrations, had stayed inside the dispatch of nearby specialists. The new designs of the NHS, nonetheless, required populace wellbeing abilities, especially in medical services arranging, and clinical officials were selected at a senior level inside these new associations. The range of abilities anyway was not the same as that expected in the customary general wellbeing job, and the current expert associations were not great fitted to support the future prerequisites of this new combination of expert jobs.

The chance to recreate the calling participated in populace medication, in whatever job, accompanied the 1974 (1973 in Northern Ireland) revamping of the NHS. It at long last united the three vital parts of clinic administrations, essential medical services, and general wellbeing in the NHS. The exchange of general wellbeing from nearby government into the NHS was not without its concerns. A large number of the MOHs went against the exchange and didn't see the value in the move of concentrate away from issues like irresistible illness, lodging conditions, instructive medication, and youngster wellbeing. All things considered, they wound up profoundly taken part in issues of medical services the executives, and were much of the time consigned to a simply warning job with restricted control over staff and assets.

The historical backdrop of general wellbeing has been a background marked by mankind's fight with illness and unexpected passing. In what is every now and again alluded to as the old general wellbeing, our initial endeavors in illness counteraction were aimed at giving admittance to clean water, safe lodging, and more nutritious and cleaner wellsprings of food, particularly meat items. We were additionally worried about issues of individual cleanliness very much delineated by our new advancement of body and hand washing, town sewerage frameworks, quarantine regulations, and populace based observation, screening, sanitization, and immunization (Greene, 2001).

For present day industrialized social orders, these actions prompted higher paces of perinatal and maternal endurance diminishes in irresistible sicknesses, and expanded future at all ages (Crimmins, 2004). After The Second Great War, sicknesses of maturing and wealth started to possess the all-important focal point of the general wellbeing plans in these countries, albeit the issues of irresistible illnesses and neediness related dismalness and mortality would keep on connecting with the wellbeing assets of non-industrial nations. These well-established examples of bleakness and mortality would likewise still canine the wellbeing and government assistance of negligible gatherings in rich countries.

Notwithstanding, during the 1980s, helped along by groundbreaking thoughts regarding wellbeing advancement, general wellbeing finished up its vision of hostile to illness general wellbeing with a correlative supportive of wellbeing vision. Sicknesses like circulatory disease (coronary failures, strokes, profound venous apoplexy, and so forth) and tumors (particularly of the gut, skin, bosom, or lung) became focuses of new types of observation, screening, and avoidance. In social orders where the nature of water, work, and lodging were amazing, individuals were viewed as gorging, exhausting, and presenting themselves to high-take a chance with substances like tobacco, liquor, asbestos, or UV radiation. Stationary ways of life had decreased fiber and expanded fat in the eating routine and diminished exercise and wellness levels. Global and working environment relocation expanded social and mental pressure as well as the longing for unsafe types of delivery. Self destruction, auto collisions, and medication related passings made sharp advances into our examples of dismalness.

This multitude of examples of way of life and disease became focuses of new avoidance and damage decrease crusades that were and remain part of so many of our new wellbeing advancement drives. The essential rule here is that wellbeing, all things considered, is our best insurance against infection and sickness. In any case, the essential point that we persistently ignore in our general wellbeing writing is that no general wellbeing drive is intended to forestall the great beyond. Everything general wellbeing strategy and practice is intended to expand the social and wellbeing administration conditions that forestall sickness and sudden passing. Our general wellbeing concerns are 'not,' nor at any point have been, a not so subtle quest for everlasting status. By the by, acknowledgment of the significant job that wellbeing advancement approaches could play in issues to do with death, biting the dust, and misfortune stays poor. Besides, when wellbeing advancement texts expound on death and misfortune they as often as possible utilize passing as a danger (see Henley and Donovan, 1999). At long last, when general wellbeing conversation goes to kicking the bucket, passing, and misfortune, these conversations are figured out as far as immediate help arrangement - clinical palliative consideration administrations or directing. Direct help arrangement isn't wellbeing advancement. The reason for this segment is to frame the job of wellbeing advancement and local area improvement thoughts and practices in the assistance of biting the dust, demise, and misfortune.

Proficient Support and Opposition

The historical backdrop of general wellbeing is loaded with pioneers whose disclosures prompted solid resistance and once in a while rough dismissal by moderate components and personal stakes in clinical, public, or political circles. Resistance to Jennerian immunization, the dismissal of Semmelweiss by partners in Vienna, and the contemporary resistance to crafted by extraordinary trailblazers in general wellbeing like Pasteur, Florence Songbird, and numerous others might discourage or defer execution of different pioneers and new leap forwards in forestalling sickness. Despite the fact that resistance to Jenner's immunization endured into the late nineteenth hundred years in certain areas, its allies step by step acquired power, eventually prompting the worldwide destruction of smallpox. These and different trailblazers drove the best approach to further developed wellbeing, frequently after severe discussion on subjects later acknowledged and which, by and large, appear to be self-evident.

Promotion has at times had the help of the clinical calling yet got a sluggish reaction from public specialists. David Marine of the Cleveland Center and David Cowie, teacher of pediatrics at the College of Michigan, proposed the counteraction of goiter by iodization of salt. Marine completed a progression of concentrates in fish, and afterward in a controlled clinical preliminary among students in 1917-1919, with startlingly certain outcomes in lessening the commonness of goiter. Cowie lobbied for the iodization of salt, with help from the clinical calling. In 1924, he persuaded a confidential maker to deliver Morton's iodized salt, which quickly became well known all through North America. Essentially, iodized salt came to be utilized in many pieces of Europe, for the most part without administrative help or regulation. Iodine-lack issues (IDDs) stay a far and wide condition, assessed to have impacted 2 billion individuals overall in 2013. The objective of global annihilation of IDDs by 2000 was set at the World Culmination for Kids in 1990, and the WHO called for widespread iodization of salt in 1994. By 2008, almost 70 percent of families in non-industrial nations consumed enough iodized salt. China and Nigeria, have had extraordinary progress as of late with compulsory salt stronghold in expanding iodization rates, in China from 39% to 95 percent in 10 years. However, the issue isn't yet proceeded to even in Europe there is lacking normalization of iodine levels and populace follow-up notwithstanding many years of figure out on the issue.

Proficient associations have added to advancing causes like youngsters' and ladies' wellbeing, and ecological and word related wellbeing. The American Foundation of Pediatrics has added to laying out and advancing elevated expectations of care for babies and kids in the USA, and to kid wellbeing universally. Clinic certification has been utilized for a really long time in the USA, Canada, and all the more as of late in Australia and the UK. It has assisted with increasing expectations of wellbeing offices and care via completing methodical companion audit of emergency clinics, nursing homes, essential consideration offices, and mental clinics, as well as walking care focuses and general wellbeing organizations (see Part 15).

General wellbeing should know about bad promotion, some of the time in light of expert traditionalism or financial personal circumstance. Proficient associations can likewise act as promoters of the state of affairs despite change. Resistance by the American Clinical Affiliation (AMA) and the medical coverage industry to public health care coverage in the USA has major areas of strength for been fruitful for a long time. The entry of the PPACA has been accomplished notwithstanding far and wide political and public resistance, at this point was supported in the US High Court and is acquiring augmenting well known help as the additional worth to a large number of previously uninsured Americans turns out to be clear. At times, the personal stake of one calling might obstruct the genuine improvement of others, for example, when ophthalmologists campaigned effectively against the improvement of optometry, presently generally acknowledged as a real calling.

Jenner's revelation of inoculation with cowpox to forestall smallpox was embraced quickly and generally. Notwithstanding, extreme resistance by coordinated gatherings of antivaccinationists, frequently drove by those went against to government mediation in medical problems and upheld by specialists with rewarding variegation rehearses, postponed the execution of smallpox immunization for a long time. At last, smallpox was killed in 1972, inferable from a worldwide mission started by the WHO. Resistance to administered limitations on confidential responsibility for weapons and handguns is extreme in the USA, drove by efficient, all around subsidized, and politically strong campaign gatherings, regardless of how much horribleness and mortality because of firearm related rough demonstrations (see Section 5).

Fluoridation of drinking water is the best general wellbeing measure for forestalling dental caries, yet it is still broadly gone against, and in certain spots the regulation has been cancelled even after execution, by efficient antifluoridation crusades. Resistance to fluoridation of local area water supplies is boundless, and viable campaigning universally has eased back however has not halted progress (see Part 6). In spite of the life-saving worth of vaccination, resistance actually exists in 2013 and hurts general wellbeing assurance. Resistance has eased back progress in poliomyelitis annihilation; for instance, revolutionary Islamists killed polio laborers in northern Nigeria in 2012, one of the last three nations with endemic poliomyelitis. Protection from vaccination during the 1980s has brought about the repeat of pertussis and diphtheria and an exceptionally huge plague of measles across Western Europe, including the UK, with additional spread toward the western half of the globe.

Headway might be hindered where all choices are made in shut conversations, not expose to open examination and discussion. General wellbeing staff working in the common assistance of coordinated frameworks of government may not be at freedom to advance general wellbeing causes. Nonetheless, proficient associations may then act as gatherings for the fundamental expert and public discussion required for progress in the field. Proficient associations, for example, the APHA give compelling campaigning to the interests of general wellbeing programs and can critically affect public arrangement. In mid-1996, endeavors by the Secretary of Wellbeing and Human Administrations in the USA united heads of general wellbeing with agents of the AMA and scholarly clinical focuses to attempt to track down areas of normal interest and readiness to advance the soundness of the populace. In Europe as well, expanding collaboration between general wellbeing associations is invigorating discussion on issues of transnational significance across the district, which, for instance, has a wide variety of guidelines on vaccination practices and food strategies.

Public backing has assumed a particularly significant part in zeroing in consideration on natural issues (Box 2.13). In 1995, Greenpeace, a worldwide ecological extremist gathering, battled to forestall the unloading of an oil rig in the North Ocean and constrained a significant oil organization to find another arrangement that would be less harming to the climate. A blast on an oil rig in the Bay of Mexico in 2010 prompted huge natural and monetary harm as well as death toll. Harms imposed on the dependable organization (English Petrol) add up to some $4.5 billion bucks and a few criminal carelessness charges are forthcoming. Greenpeace likewise proceeded with its endeavors to stop the reestablishment of testing of nuclear bombs by France in the South Pacific.

Support is a capability in general wellbeing that has been significant in advancing advances in the field, and one that occasionally puts the backer in struggle with laid out examples and associations. One of the exemplary portrayals of this capability is in Henrico Ibsen's play A Foe of Individuals, where the legend, a youthful specialist, Thomas Stockman, finds that the water locally is polluted. This information is stifled by the town's administration, drove by his sibling the city hall leader, since it would unfavorably influence intends to foster a vacationer industry of showers in their little Norwegian town in the late nineteenth hundred years.

The youthful specialist is insulted and mishandled by the residents and driven from the town, having been proclaimed an "foe of individuals" and an expected gamble. The moral story is a recognition for the man of standard who remains against the panic of the group. The term likewise took on an undeniably more evil and risky significance in George Orwell's original

1984 and in extremist systems of the 1930s to right now.

Worldwide fights prompted the discontinuance of practically all testing of atomic weapons. Worldwide worry over a dangerous atmospheric devation has prompted developing endeavors to stem the tide of air contamination from petroleum derivatives, coal-consuming electrical creation, and different indications of carbon dioxide and poisonous defilement of the climate. Progress is a long way from sure as recently enhanced nations, for example, China and India follow the rising utilization examples of western nations. Public backing and dismissal of wanton obliteration of the worldwide environment might be the best way to goad shoppers, state run administrations, and corporate substances, for example, the energy and transportation businesses to take an alternate route. The speed of progress from petroleum derivatives is slow however has caught public consideration, and privately owned businesses are looking for additional eco-friendliness in vehicles and electrical power creation, primarily however the utilization of flammable gas rather than fuel oil coal for power creation or better still by wind and sunlight based energy. The quest for "green arrangements" to the an Earth-wide temperature boost emergency has become progressively powerful, with state run administrations, the confidential area, and the overall population very cognizant of the significance of the work and the risks of disappointment.

In the last option part of the 20th 100 years and the mid-twenty-first 100 years, noticeable worldwide characters and performers have taken up causes, for example, the evacuation of hidden mortars in war-torn nations, ignorance in hindered populaces, and financing for antiretroviral drugs for African nations to lessen maternal-fetal transmission of HIV and to give care to the huge quantities of instances of Helps destroying numerous nations of sub-Saharan Africa. Rotational Worldwide plays had a vital impact in polio destruction endeavors universally. The public-private consortium Worldwide Collusion for Antibodies and Vaccination (GAVI) has been instrumental in advancing inoculation as of late, with cooperation by the WHO, UNICEF, the World Bank, the Entryways Establishment, immunization producers, and others. This critically affects stretching out vaccination to secure and save the existences of millions of kids in denied nations not yet ready to give major avoidance projects like inoculation at satisfactory levels. GAVI has carried immunizations to low-pay nations all over the planet, like rotavirus antibody, pentavalent antibody in Myanmar, and pneumococcal immunization for kids in 15 nations in sub-Saharan Africa, including DR Congo. The Bill and Melinda Doors Establishment promised US $750 million out of 1999 to lay out GAVI, with US $75 million every year and US $1 billion out of 2010 to advance the Ten years of Antibodies.

Global gatherings help to establish an overall environment of backing for medical problems. Worldwide clean gatherings in the nineteenth century were assembled because of the cholera pandemics. Worldwide meetings go on in the twenty-first hundred years to act as settings for backing on a worldwide scale, presenting issues in general wellbeing that are past the extent of individual countries. The WHO, UNICEF, and other global associations play out this job on a proceeding with premise (see Part 16). Reactions of this approach have zeroed in on the absence of comparative exertion or benefactors to address NCDs, feeble general wellbeing foundation, and that this liberates public states from liability to really focus on their own youngsters. Nobody can address, nonetheless, that this sort of try has saved innumerable lives and needs the support of other guide contributors and public government cooperation.

• Fundamental instruments of social investigation - history of general wellbeing, demography, clinical humanism and humanities, biostatistics, populace testing and overview techniques, political theory of wellbeing frameworks, standards of program assessment and wellbeing financial matters.

• Wellbeing and sickness in populaces - crucial measurements, significant human illnesses and zoonoses, the study of disease transmission of sicknesses and hazard factors, strategies for clinical analysis and counteraction, irresistible and persistent sicknesses, sustenance, climate, exceptional infection and chance gatherings, worldwide environment of infection and chance variables.

• Advancement of wellbeing and counteraction of sickness - transferable infectious prevention, constant illnesses avoidance, natural and word related wellbeing, maternal, youngster, juvenile, grown-up, and older wellbeing, emotional well-being, STI/Helps control, dietary and dental wellbeing, wellbeing training and advancement; recovery, exile, transient, and detainee wellbeing, military medication, and catastrophe arranging.

- Medical services frameworks and their administration - association and activity of public medical care frameworks, health care coverage and government backed retirement, wellbeing administrations and labor force advancement, wellbeing offices and their administration, drugs and their coordinated factors, wellbeing arranging, standards of the executives and application to wellbeing programs, planning, cost control and monetary administration, record and data frameworks, wellbeing frameworks research, wellbeing regulation and morals, innovation evaluation, certification and quality advancement in medical care, data frameworks, observing, and research techniques for the board, worldwide wellbeing.

General wellbeing arrangements to forestall corpulence can possibly be savvy because of their somewhat minimal expense and potential for long-run benefits. Notwithstanding this, an absence of proof on cost-viability and future financing slices to neighborhood experts in Britain imperils the execution of numerous preventive policies.44 In any case, nonstop spotlight on treating weight to the detriment of counteraction is probably going to bring about a thriving weight of illness and spiraling wellbeing costs from now on, particularly given the pace of expansion in heftiness in more youthful ages. While the ongoing commonness of heftiness warrants activity as treatment for corpulent people, a double methodology integrating proper preventive endeavors is important to stem the rising pattern before the interest on medical care because of weight becomes unmanageable.

Enhancing Ecological Openness Utilizing a Populace Based Approach

General wellbeing arrangements for diminishing infection can be for the most part classed as populace based systems or high-risk strategies.60, 113 the essential distinction is whether moving the whole populace dispersion of an illness or just those at the most elevated risk for disease is planned. Inventive methodologies try to target high-risk gatherings to further develop admittance to preventive intercessions. The "3 pail" conceptualization referenced prior shows how each of the three methodologies — focusing on people, focusing on high-risk gatherings, and local area wide counteraction — can cooperate to decrease the weight of sickness locally.

Local area water fluoridation is the controlled expansion of a fluoride compound to a public water supply to bring fluoride focus up to a level will best forestall dental caries while keeping away from unattractive fluorosis. It is a populace based counteraction technique that effectively moves the dispersion of dental caries locally so that more individuals are sans caries and that the people who experience caries have a decrease in the quantity of rotted teeth. Local area water fluoridation has been depicted fittingly as an exchange of epidemiologic science, science scattering, correspondence, and strategy development.4 the epidemiologic beginning with its populace wellbeing center structures the reason for general wellbeing strategy. The fluoride-caries relationship was first found in quite a while of networks with normally fluoridated water and due to this water fluoridation is the most perfect general wellbeing utilization of fluoride. Local area water fluoridation is certainly not a high-risk way to deal with caries counteraction, rather, it is populace based; its utilization implies fluoride arrives at everybody locally. This element is both the action's most prominent strength and its most prominent test regarding social approach with intrinsic difficulties of science dispersal and correspondence. The following segment examines the science intended for water fluoridation for the purpose of controlling a constant sickness, explicitly, caries at the local area level.

The unit normally utilized in the US for communicating the fluoride fixation in drinking water is parts per million (ppm), despite the fact that nations utilizing metric estimations generally express it in milligrams per liter (mg/L). Luckily, the mathematical qualities are similar in both estimating units; that is, 1.2 ppm is equivalent to 1.2 mg/L. We use parts per million in this book. As of now, our general wellbeing strategy and controls for liquor utilization are old fashioned and counterproductive. The case of supporting liquor to decrease coronary illness in high-risk populaces is demonstrative. Consequently, liquor misuse isn't ordinarily considered a medical problem but instead is viewed as a lawful and moral issue. The arrangements normally don't uphold instructing youngsters and grown-ups on the dependable use and the expected traps and dangers of liquor use, especially by those at high gamble. Most conversations center on the legitimate age for drinking and the lawful furthest reaches of inebriation. Not all around talked about are that 80% of crimes happen in the setting of liquor and that liquor use and reliance is the main gamble factor for self destruction at whatever stage in life.

In spite of these deeply grounded unfriendly results and firm information that beginning of liquor use and liquor issues happen at youthful ages, there is conspicuous promoting plainly and convincingly focused on to these high-risk populaces. Our powers over openness to liquor for weak populaces, and our schooling in rudimentary, center, and secondary schools, are horrendously lacking assuming we are to safeguard these helpless and in danger populaces. Right now, we don't consider makers of liquor responsible for the high pace of liquor related results (in the billions of dollars) because of our absence of strategy to safeguard the general population against antagonistic outcomes from liquor use.

The historical backdrop of general wellbeing strategy focuses to instances of proof informed arrangement as well as various occasions where approaches miss the mark on proof base. It very well may be contended, for example, that the evil impacts of tobacco on smoking were known during the 1950s; however strategy activity was generally negligible until the 1980s and ahead. Likewise, albeit the medical problems related with heftiness and unfortunate nourishment are very much perceived, proof informed strategy reactions are somewhat intriguing and orderly multispectral approaches are missing (Sinofsky, 2015).

Speculations about the strategy making process, which integrate acknowledgment of the legislative issues of independent direction, begin to give a few responses with regards to why proof isn't occupied all the time. There are various impacts that shape general wellbeing strategy making. Considering that the focal point of general wellbeing strategy is to drive choices helpful for society overall, there are many elements to be thought of: the ampleness and culmination of proof; the potential advantages and outcomes (and their dispersion); how to compromise present moment and long haul expenses and gains; and how to accommodate possibly clashing financial interests, social qualities, social convictions, and customs, institutional and political designs, and cycles for strategy making.

In this manner, decision-production at the populace level is many times taken in a milieu of vulnerability (Do brow et al., 2004) and it are at any point present to contend requests of partners. Networks embrace various originations of wellbeing risk (Beck, 1992), and these ideas of chance might be formed by broad communications portrayal of occasions. Media can likewise make political gamble by focusing on discusses or well-known concerns (Davies and Marshall, 2000; Marshall et al., 2005). Additionally, the discussion about arrangement decisions might be covered as clashing viewpoints about proof (Atkins et al., 2005). Leaders might be faced with both moral and educational vulnerability, as the meaning of the issue, the potential arrangements, and the idea of proof that supports both are challenged.

Moreover, strategy creators might have objectives other than adequacy with respect to wellbeing results while delivering wellbeing strategy. Wellbeing administration arrangements, which ought to at last work on clinical results, might be made with monetary, social, or key improvement objectives as a main priority (Dark, 2001). Via model, general wellbeing strategies, especially those focusing on risk factors for persistent infection, often intercede available through tax assessment or guideline. Extract charges forced on sugar-improved drinks or a scope of food varieties and refreshments considered unfortunate might fill the twofold need of diminishing utilization and raising general or wellbeing explicit income. The brief Danish duty on immersed fat substance represents the problem of such a twofold reason where the objectives are not really 100 percent harmonious: the plan of the Danish expense was viewed as bulky and strange, to some degree on the grounds that specific standards didn't appear to focus on wellbeing results, yet rather underscored expanding income assortment (Vallgårda et al., 2015). Examiners contend that the way that the expense was essential for a bigger monetary change bundle that continued through monetary instead of wellbeing dynamic designs added to its fast nullification since it permitted the political and public talk to move quickly from addressing wellbeing worries to a conversation of unfriendly financial effect and forestalled general wellbeing advocates from powerfully supporting the duty (Bødker et al., 2015; Vallgårda et al., 2015). Governmental issues, philosophy, and political economy may hence be more significant drivers of strategy making, particularly when there is logical and strategy vulnerability about the proper course of strategy activity.

Backhanded insurance and group invulnerability

For a considerable length of time, general wellbeing strategy to diminish the weight of flu in the U.S. has zeroed in on immunizing the older and people at high gamble for complexities of flu. Notwithstanding significant expansions in immunization inclusion for older and high-risk grown-ups, properly age-changed assessed yearly flu related passings have ascended at the populace level.153a For instance, the quantity of flu related passings rose from 2,265 out of 1976-1977 to 14,628 of every 1997-1998; 90% of the flu related passings happened in people ≤65 years old from 1990-1999.153b Assessed antibody inclusion for grown-ups matured ≤65 years is 66%, and 23% and 44% for high-risk grown-ups 18-49 years and 50-64 years, respectively.153c Besides, ongoing information from a very much controlled settled case control study exhibited that controlling for poor utilitarian status considerably diminishes rough antibody viability assessment in the old populace, recommending that practical status has been a significant confounder in numerous partner studies, which probably prompted the exaggeration of antibody adequacy in the elderly.153d

These perceptions have animated investigations of substitute or reciprocal inoculation procedures, including the standard immunization of kids, to forestall transmission to high-take a chance with people. 'Group resistance' is the peculiarity wherein inoculation of a high level of a populace brings about security for the people who are not immunized, as well as the people who are vaccinated.153e Various examinations have exhibited that kids enhance transmission and are basically liable for the presentation and spread of flu disease to families and in this way into the local area, recommending that immunizing youngsters could tweak local area spread.153f,153g In view of a numerical model of flu transmission, an immunization inclusion pace of 70% in kids would really cut short a local area flare-up of flu, yet lower paces of immunization inclusion of youngsters could likewise decrease the extent and effect of outbreaks.153h

The idea of crowd resistance getting from flu immunization of schoolchildren was first experimentally tried in a controlled investigation of two Michigan people group. A mediation local area (Tecumseh) in which 86% of schoolchildren was immunized with an injectable monovalent flu An immunization was contrasted with a comparable control town (Adrian). Albeit just youngsters were immunized in Tecumseh, people group wide reconnaissance showed ~60% decrease of intense respiratory diseases in the whole local area contrasted and the control town.153i The particularity of this mediation was noted when a flu B flare-up happened later in a similar season and no distinction was found in intense respiratory sickness rates in the two networks (since the immunization did exclude the B-strain).

A relationship between immunization of school-matured youngsters and decreased passings in the whole populace was found in Japan somewhere in the range of 1977 and 1987 when flu inoculation was made obligatory for Japanese schoolchildren.153j This biological review was directed reflectively. During this stretch, the nation encountered a yearly decrease of 10,000-12,000 passings from flu and pneumonia, in spite of the constraint of the immunization program to youngsters and the shortfall of a public program for old immunization. Since most flu passings happen in the old, the review writers presumed that widespread immunization of schoolchildren diminished flu related mortality in the more seasoned populace by forestalling spread of the disease to that defenseless gathering.

Information were as of late revealed from an enormous local area mediation concentrate on utilizing LAIV.153k This was an open-marked, non-randomized preliminary in youngsters to decide how much immunization inclusion of kids at the local area level could diminish spread of flu locally. Age-explicit pattern paces of medicinally gone to intense respiratory sickness (MAARI) for Scott and White Wellbeing Plan (SWHP) individuals at mediation (Sanctuary and Belton) and examination networks (Waco, Bryan, and School Station) were gotten in 1997-1998. During three resulting immunization years, youngsters (4,298, 5,251 and 5,150, individually) got one portion for each time of LAIV. Vaccinees addressed 20-25% of the age-qualified youngsters inside Sanctuary Belton. Age-explicit MAARI rates were thought about for SWHP individuals in the mediation and examination locales during the flu flare-ups. Pattern age-explicit MAARI rates per 100 people for the flu season were practically identical between the intercession and correlation networks. In the ensuing three flu seasons, grown-ups experienced decreases in MAARI rates in the mediation networks comparative with the control networks. In grown-ups >35 years old, huge decreases in MAARI of 8% (95% CI: 4%, 13%), 18% (95% CI: 14%, 22%) and 15% (95% CI: 12%, 19%), were seen in the flu seasons for immunization years

1, 2 and 3, separately. This little impact might convert into a significant impact when increased up to the populace level. Additionally this impact size might be weakened from utilization of clinical as opposed to lab endpoints. The examiners reasoned that 'immunization of roughly 20-25% of youngsters, 1.5-18 years old in the mediation networks brought about a backhanded security (crowd resistance) of 8-18% against MAARI in grown-ups >35 years old.'

As of late a limited scale pilot review followed by a bigger multi-state school-based vaccination mediation concentrate on utilizing LAIV showed the immediate and circuitous viability of this methodology. In the little pilot review, 40% of students in one primary school in Maryland were immunized with LAIV during ordinary school hours. Two comparable schools filled in as controls. All families from the three review schools were studied during the pinnacle flu episode period. Mediation school families were contrasted and control school families as the scientific structure (Table 16-9). Huge (45-70%) relative decreases in fever or respiratory disease related results including doctor visits by grown-ups, doctor visits by kids, medicine or different medications bought by family individuals, revealed family schooldays and typical business days missed were noticed for mediation ('target') school families contrasted and control school households.153l This proof of both immediate and roundabout viability was seen regardless of intraepidemic immunization during an extended period of antibody confuse. Following on this confirmation of idea, a bigger randomized bunch preliminary was directed in 28 schools gathered into 11 groups (each with 1 objective and 1-2 equivalent control schools). LAIV (FluMist®) was proposed to all qualified understudies in the objective schools, and 46% of target school understudies got LAIV. During the pinnacle flu week, target school families detailed essentially less flu like sickness (ILI)- related specialist/facility visits in youngsters, lower ILI-related remedy and nonprescription use, lower nonattendance rates for rudimentary and secondary school understudies, and less missed grown-up business days. Relative decreases across these results went from 25-40%, again affirming circuitous as well as immediate benefit.153m, 153n

In synopsis, expanding the quantity of kids immunized for flu might bring about more extensive security of the populace by means of group resistance. Investigations of different plans have shown that immunization of school-matured youngsters can bring about lower flu sickness rates in the school, the family, the local area, and everybody, apparently because of crowd resistance.

General wellbeing strategy requires cross-sectoral mediations in regions like lodging, transport, schooling, and, obviously, medical services. To address this, states are making level designs, for example, teams, cross-departmental bodies, and focal neighborhood organizations to conquer institutional deterrents to more readily handle cross-cutting issues.

In the UK, the Bureau Office Social Avoidance Team, already the Social Prohibition Unit, arranges strategy against social rejection. Perceiving that wellbeing is frequently connected to different types of rejection, a significant part of the team work on basic medical problems, for example, high school pregnancy and wellbeing disparities has tried to advance multi-organization, cross-departmental work.

The General Wellbeing Organization of Canada has a similar transmit of furnishing initiative and advancing joint effort with regions and domains on general wellbeing. The office facilitates the endeavors of bureaucratic and commonplace legislatures, the scholarly world, and nongovernmental associations to forestall persistent infections; distinguish, forestall, and lessen general wellbeing chances; and answer wellbeing emergencies.

Simultaneously, public states likewise need to arrange endeavors with nearby specialists and different legislatures at the worldwide level. Sweden gives a genuine illustration of how to advance cooperative energies between the public and neighborhood levels of government in general wellbeing (Beaglehole and Bonita, 2004). One more illustration of good practice is the Australian Public General Wellbeing Association, set up in 1996 to arrange general wellbeing drives between all degrees of government in Australia (Allin et al., 2004). For Beaglehole and Bonita, 'an ideal methodology would serious areas of strength for join moderate public rules, proper regulation and between sectoral support, with nearby drives and obligations'.

Biomedical exploration and general wellbeing arrangements commonly center on populaces. Biomedical examination endeavors to disconfirm speculations about anticipated results and, thusly, to foster realities about the reactions of creatures with specific normal attributes. Concerning logical examinations about people, gatherings are chosen for study in light of a few important natural or ecological likenesses. Any information acquired from the interaction is valuable to the degree that it is appropriate to those who share the normal condition.

General wellbeing strategies are likewise intended to affect all, and just, those people who are comparatively influenced by a sickness or a wellbeing related condition. In purposely zeroing in on some impacted gathering, biomedical science and general wellbeing strategies ordinarily give benefits just to the objective gathering. The objectives of biomedical examination and general wellbeing are distinctly aimed at everybody in the gathering which could profit from them. By glancing back at results, specialists endeavor to foster information about natural or mental responses. By looking toward the future, general wellbeing authorities endeavor to foster a generalizable way to deal with the counteraction, decrease, or treatment of natural or mental issues. Furthermore, likewise with clinical emergency in the crisis setting, biomedical exploration and general wellbeing have not been scrutinized for holding to these plans.

Since speculations of equity and thoughts regarding equity in bioethics are commonly examined each in turn, in misleadingly detached settings, and with an emphasis on painstakingly chosen models, it is difficult to see when and how their fundamental originations really conflict. However, the wide agreement on crisis emergency, general wellbeing examination, and general wellbeing strategy give an event to think about equity across an expansive range of clinical and general wellbeing settings. These models likewise challenge the supposition that an agreement upholds a solitary, fundamental rule of equity in medication and general wellbeing. As Ronald Green (2001) has noted in his analysis of Daniels, the "botch ... is attempting to choose such matters by reference to a solitary thought - and not really the main one."

Consequentialist contemplations of adequacy and balance support all around acknowledged sees on crisis emergency. At the point when the time requirements of a crisis and the requirements for clinical assets altogether surpass the accessible assets, reactions ought to be founded on viability and treating all with comparable clinical necessities correspondingly. The general rejections of emergency address the objective of keeping away from of the most horrendously terrible result. This is a fundamentally unexpected guideline in comparison to utilitarian which targets boosting the best utility. If specialists somehow managed to depend on a utilitarian standard in arranging patients in the trauma center they would initially need to make fine-grained differentiations with respect to which patients would probably experience the longest and afterward dispense treatment in view of that positioning by going down the rundown. Conversely, emergency would just reject the individuals who were most drastically averse to get by, and afterward treat every other person in view of desperation paying little heed to how long they may be supposed to live. The bases up avoidances of clinical emergency are, subsequently, not no doubt viable with utilitarianism. Nor are they predictable with either fair equity of chance or prioritarianism in light of the fact that the valuable open doors that some have and others don't and the singular distinctions that improve one individual off than one more are not considered. A portion of these various standards (stay away from the most horrendously terrible result, expand utility, fair correspondence of chance, and prioritarianism) can't be generally proper for directing similar distribution choices and ought to hence be recognized as improper for pursuing designation choices in certain circumstances.

The instincts supporting the view that need ought to be offered to balancing social chances or to giving the best advantage to the least advantaged are subverted by areas of strength for the that nonmedical relative contrasts shouldn't become an integral factor in choices about crisis reactions. This welcomes inquiries regarding the suitable structure for strategy choices about general wellbeing needs and setting the examination plan. Crisis emergency apportions assets by considering everybody's forecast and anticipated result. People absolutely get inconsistent parcels, and no need is permitted to the individuals who are all the more by and large more terrible off.

Likewise, general wellbeing research some of the time no affects the social interest, wellbeing, or life span of the whole populace. On the off chance that it just so happens, we never have another calamity like what happened on September eleventh, in the event that we at absolutely no point in the future experience a disaster that makes huge measures of crushed concrete and burned PCs and office furniture, research on their belongings might in all likelihood never advance the social cooperation or strength of anybody. Or on the other hand, assuming the weights of the intercessions that the investigations support end up being restrictively expensive (e.g., surrender high rises and PCs), they won't be embraced and nobody's fair equity of chance will be progressed. General wellbeing research includes a mission for data that could conceivably be helpful. It likewise once in a while guides assets to the requirements of somewhat scarcely any impacted people. In this way, the norms of advancing fair correspondence of chance or expanding wellbeing may not exactly fit. Assuming fair balance of chance was the main thought to be considered, numerous different purposes of assets would frequently take inclination over general wellbeing research. However, the agreement for such examination proposes that different reasons support its expansive underwriting.

Besides, while general wellbeing arrangements in some cases fulfill the guideline of advancing utility, or fair equity of chance, or need for the more regrettable off, at times they don't. In total, extensively embraced general wellbeing strategies recommend that crisis emergency, general wellbeing examination and general wellbeing strategy depend on in excess of a solitary guideline of equity.

The most significant level of proof for caries anticipation and decrease upholds the openness of teeth to fluoride. Fluoride in follow sums builds the opposition of tooth design to demineralization and is especially significant for caries counteraction (Fig. 2.42). At the point when fluoride is free during patterns of tooth demineralization, it is a main consideration in diminished caries activity.51 Fluoride is by all accounts a fundamental supplement for people and is required exclusively in tiny amounts.

Research center creatures took care of a totally sans fluoride diet foster frailty and decreased propagation after four ages. When accessible to people, fluoride produces stupendous reductions in caries frequency. The accessibility of fluoride for caries risk decrease has essentially been accomplished through the fluoridation of local area water frameworks. Fluoride openness might happen through diet, toothpastes, mouth flushes, and expert effective applications. The ideal fluoride level for public water frameworks is 0.7 mg per liter of water.52 The level of the U.S. populace with public fluoridated local area water frameworks has expanded from 62% (140 million) in 1999 to 66% (162 million) in 2000, to 69% (184 million) in 2006,23,54 to 74% (284 million) in 2014. Public water fluoridation has been one of the best general wellbeing estimates established in the US. For people group that have fluoridated water frameworks, the yearly expense midpoints about $0.70 per person.53 For each $1 spent on water fluoridation, $6 of wellbeing reserve funds are understood. The U.S. General Wellbeing Administration suggests 0.7 ppm of fluoride openly water projects to receive the rewards of water fluoridation and lessen the gamble of fluorosis. Exorbitant fluoride openness (≥10 ppm) brings about fluorosis, which at first makes veneer become white however may ultimately cause an earthy staining, a condition named mottled polish.

Fluoride applies its antiquary's impact by three distinct instruments. In the first place, the presence of fluoride particle enormously upgrades the precipitation into tooth design of fluorapatite from calcium and phosphate particles present in spit. This insoluble encourages replaces the dissolvable salts containing manganese and carbonate that was lost on account of microscopic organism's intervened demineralization. This trade cycle brings about the finish turning out to be more corrosive safe (see Fig. 2.29). Second, introductory caries sores are remineralized by a similar interaction. Third, fluoride has antimicrobial movement. In low fixations, fluoride particle represses the enzymatic creation of glucosyltransferase. Glucosyltransferase elevates glucose to shape extracellular polysaccharides, which increments bacterial grip. Intracellular polysaccharide development likewise is restrained, forestalling capacity of carbs by restricting microbial digestion between the host's feasts. In high focuses (12,000 ppm) utilized in skin fluoride medicines, fluoride particle is straightforwardly harmful to a few oral microorganisms, including MS. Concealment of development of MS after a solitary skin fluoride treatment might last a few weeks.55 It is feasible to stretch this concealment significantly by a make progress with in dietary propensities (particularly wiping out sucrose) and by the patient's honest use of a decent oral cleanliness program.

All fluoride openness strategies (Table 2.12) are compelling somewhat. Theo's clinician will likely pick the best blend for every patient. This decision should be founded on the patient's age, caries experience, general wellbeing, and oral cleanliness. Kids with creating long-lasting teeth benefit most from foundational fluoride medicines by means of the public water supply. In areas without sufficient fluoride in the water supply, dietary supplementation of fluoride is demonstrated for youngsters and some of the time for grown-ups. How much fluoride supplement should be resolved independently? This is of specific significance in provincial regions with individual wells in light of the fact that the fluoride content of well water can differ extraordinarily inside brief distances.

Effective use of fluoride ought to be done intermittently for youngsters and grown-ups who are at high gamble for caries advancement. The periodicity shifts with the case. Teeth can be cleaned free of biofilm before the utilization of effective fluorides. Flossing followed by tooth brushing is suggested for this reason. Pumicing of teeth (proficient prophylaxis) can eliminate a lot of the fluoride-rich surface layer of lacquer and might be counterproductive. Acidulated phosphate fluoride gel is viable, yet an expected gamble of gulping exorbitant measures of fluoride exists, especially in small kids. Acidulated phosphate fluoride is accessible in thixotropic gels and has a long time span of usability. Stannous fluoride (8% F), another choice, has a harsh, metallic taste; may consume the mucosa; and has a short timeframe of realistic usability. Albeit the tin particle in stannous fluoride might be answerable for staining the teeth, it might likewise be helpful in capturing root caries. Effective fluoride specialists ought to be applied by the maker's suggestions and consistently under management to restrict ingestion.

Different fluoride stains are accessible and are effective in forestalling caries. Stains give a high take-up of the fluoride particle into polish and are generally acknowledged as the vehicle of decision for fluoride conveyance to youthful grown-ups and more seasoned grown-ups the same. Fluoride stains are expertly applied and may give the most practical method for conveyance of fluoride to teeth. These stains are compelling bactericidal and caries-preventive specialists. Fluoride stains were fostered quite a few years prior trying to further develop fluoride application methods and advantages. European nations have utilized fluoride stains for a long time. Various randomized clinical preliminaries led external the US highlight the viability and security of fluoride stains as caries-preventive agents.56-64 Fluoride stain empowers the statement of a lot of fluoride on a lacquer surface, particularly on a demineralized polish surface. Calcium fluoride hastens on a superficial level, and frequently fluorapatite is framed. The high grouping of surface fluoride likewise may give a supply to fluoride, which advances demineralization. Albeit extra exploration on fluoride stains is required, the utilization of a fluoride stain as a caries-preventive specialist ought to be extended on the grounds that it enjoys upper hands over other effective fluoride vehicles regarding security, simplicity of use, and fluoride fixation at the veneer surface.6 The American Dental Affiliation (ADA) Gathering on Logical Undertakings as of late supported the utilization of fluoride-containing stains as caries counteraction agents.65

Current proof demonstrates that fluoride stains with the convergence of 5% sodium fluoride are the most effective of all topically applied fluoride products.58,66 For patients with a high gamble of caries, fluoride stain ought to be applied like clockwork. For moderate-risk patients, application at regular intervals is shown. Fluoride stain isn't demonstrated for generally safe patients.

While applying fluoride stain, the clinician gets dry spit from teeth and applies a slim layer of fluoride stain straightforwardly onto teeth. Since the fluoride stain sets while reaching dampness, careful disconnection of the area isn't needed. Just tooth brushing, instead of prophylaxis, is important before application. The primary weakness of fluoride stain is that a brief change in tooth tone might happen. Patients ought to abstain from eating for a few hours and abstain from brushing until the following morning after the stain has been applied.

Self-controlled fluoride washes make an added substance difference (around 20% decrease) when utilized related to skin or fundamental fluoride treatment. Fluoride flushes are demonstrated in high-risk patients and patients showing a new expansion in caries movement. Two assortments of fluoride washes have comparative adequacy:

(1) High portion low recurrence and

(2) Low portion high recurrence. High-portion (0.2% F)- low-recurrence washes are best utilized in managed week after week washing programs situated in government funded schools. Low-portion (0.05% F)- high-recurrence washes are best utilized by individual patients at home. A high-chance or caries-dynamic patient ought to be encouraged to utilize the wash day to day. The ideal application time is at night. The flush ought to be constrained between teeth

ordinarily and afterward expectorated, not gulped. Eating and drinking ought to be kept away from after the wash.

Routine utilization of over-the-counter fluoride containing dentifrice three times each day is suggested for all patients. These toothpastes by and large contain 0.32% sodium fluoride (1450 ppm). For moderate-hazard and high-risk patients 6 years or more seasoned, remedy dentifrices containing higher convergences of fluoride are suggested. These items normally contain 1.1% sodium fluoride (5000 ppm) and can be securely utilized something like three times each day in this age group.67 For most advantage, patients ought to be told to not flush subsequent to brushing and try not to eat or drinking for 30 minutes after use.

Sealants Are a Significant Piece of General Wellbeing Projects

With the downfall of dental caries among kids, particularly interproximal caries, sealant programs are turning out to be more proper decisions in open caries anticipation programs for youngsters. Albeit numerous dental general wellbeing drives are coordinated toward empowering the utilization of sealants in confidential practice, there is likewise significant movement in the advancement of activities to put sealants in broad daylight programs as a matter of fact. School-based sealant programs work the nation over. These projects work either in schools, generally with versatile gear, or in local area centers. The CDC reports that school-based sealant programs are an exceptionally viable method for giving sealants to the almost 7 million kids cross country who don't have them, which could forestall multiple million pits and set aside to $300 million in dental treatment costs.17 The way of thinking behind these public sealant programs is to carry this preventive technique to youngsters who in any case would be probably not going to get far reaching dental consideration. School-based and school-connected programs are focused on to schools with a high extent of youngsters from low-pay families or schools with countless kids with untreated dental requirements or to regions in which there is a lack of dentists.11 For instance, Wisconsin has encountered an expansion in school-based sealant programs throughout the course of recent years and seen a diminishing in untreated illness in 3rd grade kids thus. Also, aberrations have been wiped out and youngsters in these high-risk schools or those where more kids partake in free and diminished feast programs have higher frequency of fixed teeth than their more princely peers.75 Table 26.2 sums up refreshed suggestions for school-based sealant programs.

Assuming that the fluoride particle is integrated into or adsorbed on the hydroxyapatite precious stone, the gem turns out to be more impervious to corrosive disintegration. This response part of the way makes sense of the job of fluoride in caries avoidance, for the caries cycle is started by demineralization of polish. Clearly, in the event that fluoride is available as finish is being framed, all the polish gems will be more impervious to corrosive disintegration. How much fluoride should be controlled cautiously, in any case, in light of the responsiveness of ameloblasts to the fluoride particle and the chance of creating unattractive mottling? The semipermeable idea of veneer empowers effective application to give a higher centralization of fluoride in the surface polish of emitted teeth.

The presence of fluoride improves compound responses that lead to the precipitation of calcium phosphate. A balance exists in the oral pit among calcium and phosphate particles in the arrangement stage (spit) and in the strong stage (veneer), and fluoride moves this harmony to lean toward the strong stage. Clinically, when a restricted locale of polish has lost mineral (e.g., a white spot injury), the finish might be remineralized if the damaging specialist (dental plaque) is taken out. The demineralization response is improved extraordinarily by fluoride.

Intense poisonousness from fluoride openness at levels found in drinking water doesn't happen, however water administrators work with convergences of fluoride that are exceptionally harmful before they are weakened. Work cycles to guarantee wellbeing are followed and checked by testing of water before leaving the water plant. Rules for water administrators are deep rooted.

Confirmation of the security of ongoing openness to low degrees of fluoride has been a mainstay of general wellbeing practice, and the information base keeps on developing. For over 70 years, local area water fluoridation has fulfilled thorough logical guidelines for wellbeing. The job of fluoride in caries avoidance has developed, and various wellsprings of fluoride openness have arisen. Until this point, the gathered investigations don't show reason to worry past the unfavorable corrective impact of polish fluorosis. Endeavors to forestall veneer fluorosis at the populace level have prompted a modification of the Places for Infectious prevention and Counteraction rule for fluoride out in the open water frameworks to 0.7 ppm (mg/L). This modification addresses dynamic commitment and a cooperative methodology toward strategy improvement and confirmation in view of observation information. Joint effort between general wellbeing authorities, the dental calling, and local area partners prompted the change.

As a calling, dentistry is focused on general wellbeing. Dental experts go about as the two backers for patients and as resident researchers in their networks. These two jobs play out obviously around the subject of fluoride. In enormous measure, these jobs share a typical obligation to the moral standards of value and no maleficence — streamlining benefits and limiting dangers (see Part 3) in general wellbeing practice - guaranteeing people in general of security and further developing populace wellbeing.

Dental consideration administrations have become all the more promptly accessible to kids, and caries counteraction programs have become more viable. There has been a consistent decrease in the frequency and predominance of dental caries in long-lasting teeth among U.S. kids (see Section 10). In any case, as per the primary Top health spokesperson's report on oral wellbeing in America distributed in May 2000, dental caries is the absolute most normal constant youth disease.1 Periodontal aggravations are likewise normal. Albeit serious types of periodontal sickness are uncommon in youngsters, all involvement with least gentle gum disease once in a while. Both caries and periodontal infection are, generally, procured and preventable aggravations of the teeth and jaws. Different parts of this book are dedicated to a more top to bottom conversation of the reason, counteraction, and the board of dental caries (see Sections 10, 17, 18, and 19) and periodontal unsettling influences (see Parts 11 and 20). Wounds to the teeth and supporting tissues address one more huge classification of gained unsettling influences (see Section 21).

Numerous youngsters have orthodontic circumstances that legitimize remedial treatment, and for some of them the condition is sufficiently serious to be sorted as disfiguring or devastating. Roughly 1 of every 1000 kids in the US is brought into the world with a congenital fissure or sense of taste. These circumstances are essentially formative aggravations and are talked about more meticulously in Parts 6 and 25 to 28 26 27 28.

Endeavors to forestall viridans streptococcal disease have zeroed in on three unmistakable settings: counteraction of caries, anticipation of endocarditis, and avoidance of sepsis in neutropenia patients with malignant growth. Endeavors have been effective in the previous two settings. Nonetheless, the development of penicillin-safe viridans streptococci and worry about the conceivable rise of vancomycin obstruction feature the requirement for new ways to deal with forestall contamination with these pervasive organic entities. In growing such strategies, examiners shouldn't fail to remember that the protection from colonization gave by viridans streptococci can shield the host from additional harmful microbes (see "The study of disease transmission").

The frequency of caries in the US has been diminished pointedly by fluoridation of water supplies, consideration of fluoride in toothpaste, and adjustment of diet (e.g., utilization of sugar substitutes). Fluoride goes about as an antibacterial specialist that likewise reinforces opposition of the teeth to attack by microbes. The utilization of dental stains, gels, and washes that contain fluoride or other antibacterial specialists, for example, chlorhexidine or vancomycin might be advantageous in chosen cases.[88, 130,158,178]

The American Heart Affiliation has driven an effective work to forestall the improvement of endocarditis by fundamental anti-microbial prophylaxis of patients with known endocardia surrenders who are going through dental procedures.[58] These endeavors are pointed particularly at forestalling viridans streptococcal endocarditis, and penicillin is the anti-infection utilized most ordinarily. The system or components by which anti-toxin prophylaxis forestalls endocarditis are not seen totally. In creatures, endocarditis can be forestalled by the organization of bacteriostatic anti-microbials and by upkeep of serum levels of bactericidal anti-infection agents that are well underneath the negligible inhibitory focus for the colonizing viridans streptococci.102 Vancomycin has been seen to forestall the improvement of Vancomycin-open minded S. anguish endocarditis in tentatively tested creatures without decreasing the occurrence or level of bacteremia; hence, anti-infection agents might forestall endocarditis by diminishing bacterial adherence to endocardium.20 This speculation is upheld by a concentrate in which bacteremia, at times with anti-infection safe life forms, created in 21% of youngsters getting anti-infection prophylaxis, yet endocarditis seldom occurred.115 Notwithstanding, concentrates on in creatures have demonstrated that the likelihood of forestalling endocarditis is connected with the anti-toxin helplessness of the difficult streptococcal strains.115

Prophylaxis ought to be focused on carefully264 and managed preceding dental methodology is started. Expanded quantities of anti-infection safe viridans streptococci can be distinguished in something like 6 hours of organization of anti-microbial treatment, and they persevere for 9 days or longer.143 Exploratory investigations of the avoidance of endocarditis by the organization of anti-microbials after challenge with bacterial inoculate have yielded conflicting results,22,125,152 and the clinical utility of this approach isn't known.

As of late, viridans streptococcal contaminations have turned into a significant issue in neutropenic patients with malignant growth and in beneficiaries of bone marrow transfers. Since penicillinresistant viridans streptococci are boundless, some disease habitats remember vancomycin for the underlying empiric anti-toxin routine for neutropenic patients with unexplained fever.235 likewise, in spite of worry about the chance of prompting vancomycin-safe bacterial strains, doctors overseeing bone marrow relocate units are directing intravenous vancomycin prophylactically to high-gamble with patients with an end goal to forestall the advancement of viridans streptococcal sepsis; the consequences of an observational associate review support this practice.124

Two no controlled preliminaries of oral vancomycin paste15 or vancomycin mouthwash37 in kids who were getting cytotoxic chemotherapy proposed viability in the counteraction of viridans streptococcal contamination. Nonetheless, expanded colonization and contamination with vancomycin-safe enterococci are an anticipated outcome of expanded vancomycin use, which has incited the Habitats for Infectious prevention and Counteraction (CDC) to suggest that empiric vancomycin treatment be kept away from when practical and has driven specialists to investigate options in contrast to the empiric or prophylactic utilization of vancomycin.

In a similar preliminary, penicillin prophylaxis was better than TMP-SMX prophylaxis in forestalling viridans streptococcal contaminations in patients with malignant growth in spite of broad colonization with penicillin-safe streptococci.109 In different examinations, oral organization of penicillin or roxithromycin, a macrolide anti-infection, likewise seemed to diminish the rate of viridans strep to coccal disease in patients with malignant growth in contrast with verifiable controls.61,215,244 conversely, in an investigation of prophylactic organization of ampicillin to patients getting autologous bone marrow transfers, no decrease in the frequency of viridans streptococcal sepsis happened, though the occurrence of penicillin opposition increased.26 Expanded penicillin obstruction related with penicillin prophylaxis has been noted in other prophylactic preliminaries as well.244 The CDC doesn't suggest the standard utilization of penicillin prophylaxis in patients getting bone marrow transplants.108

Levofloxacin prophylaxis presently is involved normally to forestall bacterial contaminations in grown-ups with disease, yet viridans streptococci quickly create quinolone obstruction, a place of concern.261 Imaginative prophylactic techniques and painstakingly planned clinical preliminaries are expected to distinguish compelling prophylactic measures, particularly for patient companions at high gamble, for example, youngsters getting chemotherapy for intense myeloid leukemia.

Albeit many water supplies contain some normally happening fluoride, changing the fluoride focus to the ideal level for caries counteraction is an exceptionally compelling technique for forestalling and controlling the impacts of the dental caries process. The primary change of water fluoride levels in the US happened in Great Rapids, Michigan, in 1945. 25 states and the Locale of Columbia have met or surpassed the national objective of 75% of the U.S. populace served by local area water frameworks with ideally fluoridated water.15 In 2000, 65% (MMWR July 11, 2008), and in 2008 almost 70% of U.S. occupants utilizing water from a shared water framework approached fluoridated water.16 Accomplishing more significant levels of fluoridation are supposed to require

(1) acknowledgment by strategy creators and the public that dental caries stays a significant general medical condition and that fluoridation is an impartial and financially savvy technique for resolving the issue, even in more modest populaces where the per-capita cost of fluoridation is higher;

(2) proceeding with science-based training of people in general about the laid out security of fluoridation;

(3) the political will to embrace new fluoridation frameworks in networks that are not as of now served. To conquer the difficulties confronting fluoridation, general wellbeing experts at the public, state, and nearby levels should improve their advancement of fluoridation and commit the important assets for gear, faculty, and preparing.

The advantages of fluoride openly water frameworks as well as in a wide assortment of definitions and conveyance vehicles are by and large acknowledged by the general wellbeing local area, dental scientists, and rehearsing experts worldwide.56,102,105 This part presents an outline of the job of fluoride in forestalling dental caries. It sums up material from precise audits and clinical proposals distributed by boards who created proof based rules. The peruser is urged to follow these sources since refreshes happen regularly, and new proof is regularly incorporated into our insight base for fluoride.

The section starts with an unthinking perspective on fluoride in caries counteraction then portrays the manners in which avoidance can be custom-made to address wellbeing across various settings starting with the populace level and afterward zeroing in on clinical dental practice uses of fluoride before at long last growing past the conventional dental work on setting to address high-risk bunches beyond the dental clinical utilizing imaginative ways to deal with broaden anticipation.

The exceptional remedial antiquary's impact of fluoride is presently perceived to be fundamentally interceded by its post eruptive (effective) collaboration with the tooth structure. Early observational examinations recognized a job for fluoride in lacquer development in light of a condition known as dental fluorosis (see Part 24). This prompted examinations that zeroed in on fluoride reactivity with tooth mineral and its consolidation into the creating tooth structure, which frames a more steady mineral stage, known as fluorapatite, subsequently diminishing corrosive dissolvability and forestalling dental rot. Notwithstanding, the previous accentuation on the significance of fluoride consolidation during tooth development (its preeruptive impact) has been eclipsed by later examinations, and it is currently commonly acknowledged that the posteruptive (effective) connection of fluoride with the tooth structure represents by far most of fluoride's antiquaries benefit.66 At suggested levels in drinking water, fluoride gives a minimal expense, consistent state foundation level of security that moves the dispersion of dental caries in a good way for a whole local area.

Over-the-counter (OTC) oral consideration items, bought by people, have fluoride levels at focuses adequate to enter the dental biofilm that structures on tooth surfaces, conveying helpful degrees of fluoride to the polish and all the more critically packing fluoride in early sores. Generally, people group water fluoridation at the populace level and OTC oral consideration items with fluoride at the singular level are adequate for caries counteraction for some people. Nonetheless, for a few high-risk gatherings and people, designated approaches can be useful. This part features the manners in which that fluoride can be utilized in various definitions and in a scope of settings to forestall dental caries. For every fluoride methodology, there is a biomechanical setting for successful conveyance of the fluoride specialist as well as a strategy cultural setting. The point is to furnish the peruser with information to help viable choices for dental caries avoidance utilizing fluoride modalities.

The oral medication clinical practice rules distributed by the SSF suggest the utilization of a high-strength skin fluoride (any structure) for caries prevention.20 Fluoride is liable for the development of fluoroapatite gems inside the tooth structure, which are more impervious to corrosive assault and disintegrate at a lower pH of 4 than the hydroxyapatite precious stones (pH 5.6) in tooth polish. Fluoride likewise goes about as an impetus for the remineralization of the tooth surface within the sight of supersaturated calcium and phosphate typically found in unstipulated spit. Day to day utilization of OTC fluoride washes (500 ppm), customary toothpaste with fluoride (1000-1200 ppm), or original potency fluoride gels (5000 ppm) forestalls the arrangement of new rot and advances remineralization in the beginning phases of rot. On the other hand, fluoride stain (22,500 ppm) applied on the teeth like clockwork by a dental expert likewise gives a successful method for caries prophylaxis. The recurrence and sort of fluoride application is reliant upon the patient's gamble, seriousness, and involvement in different medicines.

www.ingramcontent.com/pod-product-compliance
Lightning Source LLC
LaVergne TN
LVHW010106170225
803897LV00015B/1609